William Coke Harrell, MD

CAROLYN CONGER, PHD, is a consultant and teacher who conducts seminars internationally in psychological growth, dream work, intuition, creativity, and spirituality. She has lived with tribal societies throughtout the world, studying their healing and metaphysical arts. From her research in psycho-immunology and her experience of working with people with illness, she also teaches mind/body techniques for attaining optimum wellness. Her doctorate is in clinical psychology.

D0029587

Through the Dark Forest

Transforming Your Life in
the Face of Death

Carolyn Conger, PhD

ℙ

A PLUME BOOK

PLUME
Published by the Penguin Group
Penguin Group (USA) LLC
375 Hudson Street
New York, New York 10014

USA | Canada | UK | Ireland | Australia | New Zealand | India | South Africa | China
penguin.com
A Penguin Random House Company

First published by Plume, a member of Penguin Group (USA) LLC, 2014

LIBRARY OF CONGRESS CATALOGING-IN-PUBLICATION DATA

Conger, Carolyn.
  Through the dark forest : transforming your life in the face of death / Carolyn Conger, PhD.
    pages cm
  Includes bibliographical references and index.
  ISBN 978-0-452-29870-5
  1. Death—Psychological aspects.   2. Thanatology.   I. Title.
  BF789.D4C657 2014
  155.9'37—dc23

                                        2013022731

Printed in the United States of America
10 9 8 7 6 5 4 3 2 1

Set in Bembo Book MT Std

In loving memory of

Judy Conger Calder

Michael Crichton

William Brugh Joy

We're all just walking each other home.

—RAM DASS

CONTENTS

ACKNOWLEDGMENTS

Heartfelt thanks!

To my clients and friends who shared themselves and their process during the past thirty-five years and taught me all I know about transformational work with the dying. To my family, friends, and clients who were supportive and patient during the months of writing this. To everyone in the field of thanatology—from researchers and writers to hospice workers and compassionate caretakers, who have served the needs of the dying and contributed to the growing body of knowledge about end-of-life care. To my niece, Kim Calder, magnificent inspiratress, who offered suggestions, edited, and cheered me through the rough spots. To Coke Harrell, MD, for his love, suggestions, and clarification of medical matters. To Brandon Lees, physical trainer and friend, who keeps me healthy. To Clare Ferraro, at Penguin, who invited me to write this book, and to all the staff there, who were caring and responsive. To my editor at Plume, Becky Cole, who polished my writing and taught me so much. Finally, thanks to Captain Jean-Luc Picard and the crew of the starship *Enterprise*, who provided me with a model of discipline I sorely needed to complete this project.

INTRODUCTION

In the midpoint of this journey that is our life I
found myself passing through a dark forest, the
right path through which had disappeared. And
what a hard thing it is to speak of that savage
forest. . . .

—Dante, *The Divine Comedy*

Dante's poem, describing his difficult journey through a dark
forest without a path to follow, inspired the title of this
book. It is an accurate description of the dilemma in which
many people at the end of life find themselves. And the experience can indeed be savage. Knowing they have only a few
weeks, months, or years to live, they suddenly are forced to
grapple with important issues. If you are a person with a terminal or increasingly debilitating illness, you probably are struggling with these questions:

- How can I leave this world with a sense of peace and
  grace?
- How do I want to die?
- How will my loved ones remember me?
- How can I get through the pain and suffering at
  the end?
- Is there anything more to learn at this stage of my
  life?

- Who am I now—and how can I find meaning at the end of my life?
- Is there anything unfinished I need to attend to?
- How can I heal my broken relationships before I leave?
- Are there tools or techniques for getting through all this?
- What psychological and spiritual resources are available to me now?
- Is there anything redemptive about this time before death?

These are difficult questions. And it is natural for you to ponder them over and over. Something in us wants to have a satisfactory sense of completion to our time upon this earth. Every story has a beginning, a middle, and an end. The more we participate in writing the ending of our own story, the more satisfied we are with the arc of our life.

∼

This book is an attempt to help you with these inquiries about the end of life. It draws upon my experience of working with people who are facing death. It contains examples of how I work with them psychologically and spiritually during this critical time, and presents suggestions and exercises for the reader to explore. It is not only for people who have a terminal illness and for their caretakers and families, but also for everyone who is ready to face their own mortality and live the remainder of their lives meaningfully, no matter how long that may be.

In these pages are stories about my clients and friends—excerpts from my notes and recordings—about their struggles and victories and how we worked together to make their remaining time transformative.

Personal transformation is much more than change; it's a radical rearrangement, reintegration, and renovation of consciousness that sweeps through our being much like the metamorphosis of a butterfly's life cycle. It is so powerful that it affects body, mind, and spirit. When it happens, others see us as reborn, and we in turn experience and interact with the world differently—with an expanded viewpoint, from a place of wholeness. We feel more "ourselves" than ever before.

This is not a religious or philosophical book about death and dying, but rather a practical self-help guide to doing inner psycho-spiritual work when it is most needed. Each chapter contains some of the techniques that will help this process unfold.

In the Western world, death and the dying process have been erased from the cycle of life.

We try not to talk about it or think about our own death. Rarely is it a topic for family discussions. Our high schools and colleges teach about the life cycles of animals and plants, and though they offer courses in human development, little, if anything, is taught about the final stages of human life. In hospitals, great care is taken to conceal a dead patient's body so the other patients won't know someone has died. And the field of geriatrics only recently has begun to focus on end-of-life issues. If you need further evidence that we are in denial about death, consider the fact that we hire a person to put makeup on our deceased for a "viewing" before burial or cremation.

We need to quit sanitizing death, trying to keep it invisible and quiet in the back rooms of hospitals and skilled nursing facilities. We need to stop talking about an individual's path to the end of life in whispers because we do not know how to be with them or what to say to them.

The critical moment when death becomes a personal reality—usually when a medical professional delivers the news of an end-stage disease—can be an initiation into a profound and meaningful process of personal transformation. It is a unique opportunity to learn and grow into the essence of one's true self. It is, in some ways, equivalent to a birth announcement. Realizing that we have a finite period of time on this earth, our whole being wakes up. We become mobilized, eager to make our remaining time count, to find meaning and purpose. For many, it is an experience of rebirth and renewal, even with the concurrent feelings of fear.

We need guidance for this difficult traverse, and we need companions who are not afraid of being with disease, suffering, or death, who can create a safe environment for this exploration. We need support. I believe end-stage illness is a unique, sacred experience that can foster meaningful growth, and I would like to help you to learn how to unfold into your wholeness.

For thirty years I have had the privilege of working with people who know their death is imminent. Some come to me in terror, others in hope of a miracle, and most feel confused by the medical maze. All want assistance navigating the dilemma of still being alive yet constantly forced to consider and prepare for the cessation of life. While this is a dilemma we all face, the immediacy of death associated with a terminal illness brings us closest to one of the most puzzling aspects of being human— the fact that we are conscious we will die. At first this sudden challenge is incomprehensible, especially to those who don't feel or look sick. Immediately, all that is superfluous in life falls away. Their attention becomes riveted on one thing: I am going to die.

The knowledge of this ending is weighed down by the anticipation of great suffering and pain, brought on by portrayals of terminal illness in books or movies and echoed in the faces of family and friends.

My clients who are at the end of life often enter a dark forest. As they traverse the unsteady path, not knowing what creature will cross their way or what deep chasm blocks their passage, obstacles and horrors confront them. The usual coping skills for survival and techniques for seeking well-being don't work in this uncharted territory. And who will help them?

My first experiences working with mental and physical illness occurred when I was in my twenties. As a probation officer with a caseload of drug addicts, I learned firsthand the realities of physical deterioration, and how to be with people for whom the possibility of dying was a daily reality. One year I also worked on weekends as an occupational therapist at a rehabilitation center, where I had been hired to teach reading to quadriplegic male patients in the spinal cord unit. Some patients were affected by brain trauma, while others had never learned to read. I began to work with them using creative visualization, which they found relieved the boredom of lying in bed all day. I was greatly surprised to discover these techniques also often alleviated much of their mental and physical discomfort.

Death was very much present in the facility as well. I remember two of these men in particular, who said they wanted to die. Week after week, my greatest challenge was to help them discover inspiration for living on their own terms.

When I later began teaching workshops and consulting in the field of transpersonal psychology—a full-spectrum approach that includes transcendent experience—it seemed as though someone had erected a neon sign over my office that read, IF YOU ARE ILL—COME ON IN! And many did come, with a wide variety of health challenges and needs. I soon realized that the individuals who came to me with terminal illness required a special approach.

In 1976, I became involved with the pioneering Center for the Healing Arts, one of the first holistic health training centers in the United States. There I discovered others who were interested in working with people with illness in ways that complemented my own ideas. It was the dawn of a new age in psychology and alternative medicine. Dr. Hal Stone, the founder, developed programs for cancer patients. I taught dreamwork and intuition, and these people for whom death was a reality, not an abstraction, shared their lives with us wholeheartedly. From them we learned about the concerns and needs of people who were facing death. Mainly, I learned that support from family, friends, and health care practitioners was the most important factor in helping a person at the end of life, and that this support should be tailored to each individual's desires. In other words, the client chooses how that support will happen.

I have also been fortunate to experience different approaches to death in my time with various indigenous cultures around the world. Living with the Dayak tribe on the Mahakam River in southeast Borneo, for example, revealed how death claims her due from animals, humans, and the jungle itself. There I saw life feeding on life—openly. Young boar were ceremoniously killed in front of us for our welcoming feast. Through my binoculars I saw a crocodile capture a heron and take it underwater, and witnessed a snake kill what appeared to be a baby monkey. There were howls in the night from a pack of wild dogs who had made their kill. And because this process felt rooted in nature, it was acceptable to me. Each night when we arrived at a new village we would climb a steeply inclined log, slippery and without notches, from the canoe on the river to the community longhouse, elevated on high stilts. As I tested each step, I could feel death riding my left shoulder. She was always present, a necessary partner of the life force throbbing in the jungle.

Through being with my friends on the Hopi reservation, in addition to other tribes in the Arctic, Africa, South America, and many other places, I learned the importance of preparing for death and entry into the afterworld. Each tribe's mythology and ritual practice is unique, and yet there is a similarity in the attitude about letting go. All of these cultures honored the process of dying as a valuable part of a natural cycle. They interacted with the force or personage of death through masks, dance, ritual, story, and celebration.

Yet, I believe it was my own history of surviving several serious illnesses that initially sparked my interest in better understanding death and in working with ill people. Paralyzed for several years during my late teens with encephalomyelitis, I underwent a difficult recovery, moving from total dependence on medical assistance to eventually walking on my own again. When I finally graduated to a wheelchair, I was told this would be the extent of my recovery. Physical therapy was not available to me at the time. But I was determined to walk again, and exercised by using soup cans I had tied in a pillowcase as weights. I practiced imagery by envisioning myself running and playing volleyball. I had my friends tip me out of my wheelchair onto the sand at the beach, and tried to crawl as I visualized myself crawling all the way to the ocean. My experience taught me how important the psychological process is in healing. I learned about patience, resolve, discipline, and the power of imagery and imagination. On my own, I explored what today we call the "mind-body connection."

My journey with illness didn't end there. In my thirties, I almost died from an ectopic pregnancy. Lying in the hospital bed for weeks, I went in and out of liminal states of consciousness, experiencing visions and visitations that seemed not of this world. I found that death was nothing to fear, and that it would be easy to let go when the time came.

Later in life, I again learned to appreciate the thin veil that separates life and death when I contracted a chronic lung disease and was constantly confronted with the terror of being unable to breathe. It took me two years to recover fully.

These experiences revealed to me that my intuitive wisdom was just as vital as the conventional medical treatment I received, and that both could guide the course of healing. I came to believe that as much as I wanted to regain full physical function, whether I was able to do so did not matter as much as becoming whole psychologically and spiritually. I came to define healing as *moving toward wholeness*. I believe that transformation into wholeness is a person's true work, and that this work can take place over a lifetime or in the few days or hours preceding death.

Usually, moving into your wholeness involves shifts in how you see yourself, as well as behavioral changes. Hopefully, we'll spend our whole lives discovering who and what we are, and what our potentials are. We are creatures designed for growth and self-discovery; some say this is our purpose for being on this earth. For those of you who are facing death, time itself is inviting you to explore your deepest essence, to delight in what you find as you practice the exercises in this book. I hope you'll be pleasantly surprised with what you discover, and that when you uncover aspects of yourself that are difficult—which we all have—you'll be gentle and nonjudgmental.

∽

When people with a terminal illness are referred to me, I say I will take their hands and walk with them through all the challenges their illness presents. I tell them we will discover gifts along the way, hidden gold in their dreams and relationships they've not attended to, unfulfilled longings, creative expressions, new experiences and ways of being. We embark on an exploration of their deep psyches, of the meaning of their lives. I tell them I will do my best to be with them at the end, if they wish. It's not an easy process, but it can be incredibly fulfilling, as it was with my young client Maurice.

Maurice was a teenager who was in the end stages of leukemia. His parents brought him to me because they thought he needed an experienced person to talk to about his impending death. We met weekly for several months and texted almost every day. We explored his fears and questions about the dying process and a possible afterlife. I helped him grieve about missing out on having a girlfriend, experiencing sex, becoming a parent, and having a job. I taught him meditation and techniques for pain relief. He became very good at dreamwork, and got fully engaged in "decoding" his dreams. When he was semiconscious in the hospital, the day before he died, he told me he thought dying was like going to sleep and waking up in another dream.

My goal for all my clients is to invite them to see this stage of transition as an initiation into a profound and meaningful process of personal transformation, an opportunity to learn and grow into the essence of who they truly are. I tell them just because death is probably imminent, it doesn't mean the journey is over. In fact, this might be the most exciting part of their lives. Some open to a feeling of connection to all of life, or a guiding presence in the universe.

A few enter kicking and screaming, but eventually, most choose the transformative path. It is the best choice. They realize the special possibilities that are opened by their mortality.

The scope of my service may include contact with family members, medical personnel, clergy, and others. But most of the work is done with the individual. We may meet only a few times, or it may be an ongoing relationship that lasts several months or even years.

On their path to wholeness, we struggle, grieve, question, and celebrate their discoveries together. Most come to accept that their lives are going to end, and that they can choose how to be and what to do with the time they have left. It is never too late for transformation.

I offer here the example of two of my friends who have battled the challenge of cancer for several years, and who have faced the fact of their mortality. I asked each to tell me about her process and why she thinks she has been able to endure the rigors of the disease and continue her personal growth work throughout the experience.

   The first friend I'd like to share some wisdom from, Nami, is a renowned educator in Japan, who facilitates psychological trainings. She is a Harvard-trained physician who has chosen to focus on the psycho-spiritual aspects of learning and healing, rather than the practice of medicine. She wrote me this e-mail in answer to my query about her process a few months ago. Her responses were so beautiful, I've simply asked her permission to share them with you here.

   Hi Carolyn,

   I have been contemplating the question of how I've coped with my illness of the past three years. Thank you for the question. I came up with the following so far:

   I am self-aware much of the time.

   I am fairly honest, and do not kid myself with excuses, reasons, or explanations.

   I do not fear the dark side of myself or the world, although I haven't encountered it much, and have integrated a lot of it.

   Being sick does not bring me much payoff, and the cost of it is too great.

   I am intentional, strong willed, curious about and interested in a lot of things, and am independent.

   I take responsibility for my life and the way it is.

   I prefer to be healthy and active.

And I know about surrendering a bit.

I took responsibility for being ill, and took a stand to be well.

I am willing to be healed of past events.

I am not afraid to change (I think).

It was an interesting time to come up again against death—perished, annihilated, being no more. The fear is beyond my volitional control, I found. I could, however, stand outside my panicky, frightened ego a little bit more than before. I'd say the meditation practice helps with this. I also found that I was reacting to my reactions, and was not present to the experience of fear or any other experience of the moment itself. That was sort of an amazing thing to find.

My other friend's name is Hope. She's a painter, and loves spending time with her grandchildren. Since she was diagnosed with cancer five years ago, she has had four surgeries and two rounds of chemotherapy, and is currently undergoing Cyber-Knife robotic radiosurgery, which delivers beams of high-dose radiation to tumors.

She has been doing transformational work during the time she's been ill, and says not only that it has brought about great changes in her life but also that she can't imagine coping with her illness without these tools for inner growth. Hope says that since she contracted cancer and has been "doing the work," she has become a better human being. Here is the list she gave me when I asked her about the results of her experience:

My spirituality has deepened.
Every birthday is a celebration.

I am mindful, superconscious—but not personally self-conscious.

I am self-aware, and more compassionate.

I am "real" now, with authentic integrity. No deceit or defense.

I appreciate every day, and live in the present.

I love my scars.

I haven't been afraid, not even of death.

I feel fully embodied; I meditate to be present.

I know that forgiveness simply means, "move on and walk love."

I believe that God chooses people to show faith through illness.

I'm whole now, feel love in my heart. This is my truth.

These two women glow when they talk about what they've gained by doing transformational work. They and others tell me that the presence of death that accompanies them through their days adds energy and vitality to their daily experience. It makes life sharper and more immediate—every moment counts.

This book is for those of you who are entering the dark forest, and for your friends, family members, and caretakers who will accompany you. Your illness may have initiated existential dread, but you are not alone: Every one of us has a terminal illness, because our bodies are not immortal in the world. Consciousness may continue, but the space we inhabit on earth will end.

As you read through these pages, you will need a journal to do the exercises, track your progress, and record your thoughts, images, and feelings. Your writing is an important part of the exercises, because it embodies and grounds your experience.

My wish is that this book will show you that you're not alone, help you find purpose and hope, and help you discover what within you wants to be born.

Through
the
Dark
Forest

CHAPTER I

Engage with Your Life

Death is the mother of beauty, mystical.
—Wallace Stevens, "Sunday Morning"

If you are facing death, the most important thing you can do is to engage with your life. This means examining everything about it with fresh eyes, discovering what has meaning and value for you, and healing the places where you are out of balance. Then, when your time on earth is finished, you can surrender to death with a sense of completeness, knowing you've fulfilled what mattered. This is profound, psycho-spiritual work that accompanies the physical challenges and treatments you may be involved with. It is healing work with the heart and mind. This moving toward wholeness is a process that is open, fluid, and unique for each individual. It takes courage to do this work.

The central goal of my work with people, whether they are ill or not, is to help them attain wholeness. What is wholeness? It is not the same for everyone, but it always involves growth toward being all of who you can be—to become the truest version of who you really are. This means that we recognize, get to know, and honor all aspects of ourselves. Becoming whole does not mean we are striving toward an ideal or perfection. On the contrary, we are open to discovering new things about ourselves that may be tiny seeds that need nourishment to grow. For example, if you are a person who focuses on hard work to the exclusion of play in your life, you are not in balance. The energies of work and play are complete opposites, and ideally, you would value and make time for each. When we are out of balance, our bodies and minds are not operating harmoniously. This creates tension, which affects our physical and mental health.

Becoming whole also means that we learn to experience our deepest essence, the part of consciousness that is beyond language, thought, personal identity, and time. We become pristine awareness, energetically connected to everyone and everything in existence. Some relate this to the concept of soul or spirit. Practicing meditation is one way to contact our essential state of being.

You'll find many stories in these pages of people who have discovered neglected or new aspects of themselves, or who have identified habits and attitudes that have caused unhappiness and problems. Looking at these challenges objectively without beating up on ourselves is the first step. Choosing and utilizing a resource to create the transformation to wholeness is the second step. And finally, practicing the new behavior or attitude or engaging the discovered aspect of self is the third step.

Sometimes we are so accustomed to habitual ways of seeing ourselves that it's difficult to incorporate the positive aspects that we discover, but because we are all inherently hungry for growth and learning, our natural tendency propels us into the new experience of wholeness. Unconsciously, we yearn to embrace what has been undeveloped or excluded.

Here are two examples. Peter was a client of mine who grew up in a military family. He related to people as if he were a commanding officer in the Marines. He approached them in a stiff, formal manner and never shared his vulnerability. His speech was clipped, with a sharp tone, and he rarely loosened up or laughed. This precluded an intimate connection to those he cared about, and consequently he didn't keep friends for very long. He felt lonely and isolated, and didn't understand why his friends always drifted away. Attaining wholeness for him meant learning to approach others with an open, easy manner and dropping his military posture, which was his defense against vulnerability.

The word *vulnerability* is a psychological concept that means someone is open to his or her feelings, self-discovery, new experiences, and ways of interacting with the world. A person open to his vulnerability has a fluid relationship with others, and doesn't need always to be in control. He is eager to learn useful coping mechanisms. It does not mean weakness. Peter learned to incorporate other parts of himself that were more naturally expressive and responsive to other people. It took a while, but he gradually learned to relate to others in a gentle, open way. After a year of dedicated inner work and intentional behavioral changes, he enjoys the friendships he has cultivated. Also, he met his special woman and is now married to her.

Another client, Anne, came to me because she was experiencing depression. A successful businesswoman, she was the CEO of an international textile company. At age forty-three, she was plagued with incapacitating migraine headaches, which caused her to lose days of work.

Rather than rest when these occurred, she would try to

power through and direct her staff from home. Of course, this made the headaches worse and frustrated her even more. Once she embarked on her journey of self-discovery, she was amazed to realize that she had let go of an important part of her natural self—her creativity. The love of creating textile patterns was what initially got her into the textile business. Through working with her dreams and imagery, she realized that she missed the joy of laying out a design, working with color, and the feel of the completed cloth in her hands. Her job as CEO did not bring her the same pleasure. She kept her CEO position, but started contributing textile designs and spending time on the factory production line regularly. Anne reclaimed her creative side, bringing herself into balance and wholeness, and the migraines stopped.

These are simple examples of profound transformation that can occur when we engage with our lives.

My philosophy is that life presents each of us with particular challenges, such as illness, and we can take the opportunity to learn skills that will aid us in surmounting those challenges. No matter the length of time you have to live, the greatest gift you can give yourself is to explore the unknown and imbalanced aspects of your being and bring them into wholeness, while at the same time deepening your connection to the spiritual essence that is at the core of your being and in all life.

Here's an exercise that will help you begin to discover how you view your life today. It will give you direction for beginning or deepening your inner work. Something magical happens when we take the time to write regularly in our journals: We train our minds to focus on what's important, resulting in a clear expression of needs, solutions, and resources of which we may be unaware. We also create a relationship with the deeper wisdom, or intuition, within ourselves that is always available. The more we write in our journals with the intention of opening to our intuition, the easier it becomes to connect to it, and the more easily it flows.

Exercise: Life Portrait

Open your journal to a blank page. Read through the following questions and then sit comfortably with your eyes closed. When you feel ready, open your eyes, pick up your pen, and begin to write without censoring. Write in detail until you feel finished with each question. Trust that your inner wisdom will present you with valuable truth.

1. Do I feel broken anywhere in my life? If so, where?

2. Are there relationships I'm ready to heal?

3. Where have I been successful?

4. What makes me happy?

5. Where do I feel incomplete?

6. If I were guaranteed five more years to live, what would I choose to do or change?

7. How do I want to live in the time I have left?

8. Is there any action I'm inspired to take now? Pick the time and place to put one of your insights into action, which is moving toward wholeness.

9. You may come back to these questions in a few days, then weekly. Review your previous answers and see

what you can add to them. Perhaps you'll have realizations and ideas about what more you can put into action, or what changes you can make in your life during the next week.

Heal your difficult relationships

Almost all people who are approaching death want to correct broken relationships that have compromised their sense of harmony with another person, a family, or a community. It's one of the most important tasks to accomplish before we leave this earth. Harmonious relationships bring us nourishment, security, and joy. They are the cornerstone of a life lived well, and a major part of our wholeness.

Here is an example of one of my clients who struggled with the relationships she had with her family, friends, and people at work. When she became ill with cancer, her problems with relationships increased.

At fifty-eight, Jane was divorced, had three grown children with whom she had minimal contact, and lived alone in a large house that was important to her. For twenty years she had worked in a private mental health clinic, finally becoming the chief psychiatrist and now the administrative director. She loved her work and was at the clinic at least fifty hours a week. "Even with all the problems of serving a low-income clientele, I'd rather be there working than doing anything else," she said.

She revealed to me that two years ago she had her first

chemotherapy for metastatic breast cancer. The disease had spread to her bones. She received several more rounds of chemo, but none was effective and the cancer continued to infiltrate. She also received radiation, but nothing stopped the growth of the cancer. Although she had disease throughout her body, she had no symptoms and felt well, proudly describing her long hikes in the mountains and her strong tennis serve. She said it was strange to feel normal and energetic, and at the same time know logically she was approaching death. It was worse being a physician, she said, because she knew the statistics, and they were dismal. "Why do my markers keep going up?" she almost shouted. "I'm a good person and this shouldn't be happening to me." She continued railing about her bad luck, naming a plethora of incidents in her life she found unfair, repeating several times that no one liked her and that she was lonely.

"I think my father was right," Jane said. "I'm just not good enough. He said I was only average, so I spent my life trying to please him and prove him wrong. I worked my butt off in medical school to be at the top of the class and read everything I could to be intelligent enough for him. He didn't live long enough to see me graduate. I've done well at work, but the rest of my life is terrible—I'm lonely, don't have close friends, and I long for a love relationship with a man. My marriage was miserable, but I'm ready to try again—pretty hopeless at fifty-eight, isn't it? Who would want me now, with cancer?" Jane laughed bitterly. She believed she was responsible for her own illness—that some psychological or spiritual deficiency, or an action that she'd failed to complete, had caused her malady. In her words, she'd "screwed myself up," and she believed the only path to finding peace was for a miracle to cure her cancer, so she could go back and fix everything.

Many people who are faced with the end of their lives aren't pleased with the prospect of the end, and they discover they're dissatisfied with what's come before it. They feel like they've failed in living the life they wanted. You may be thinking that you never succeeded in having a good relationship, or that you failed to complete your dream of creating your own business. I have a friend who was devastated when he heard the news that his illness was incurable and he had only months to live. More than the prospect of death itself, he was upset by the fact that he hadn't "made it" in the music business, and saw himself as a failure. And he was concerned that his children too would remember him as a failure.

Stay connected to others

Family members in particular are stunned when dark emotions from the shadow side of their loved one's personality come out when they are ill. Physical pain and discomfort, confinement to home or bed, and diminished social contact amplify the shadow, pushing one deeper into the dark forest, causing one to feel alone. This is a natural defense that brings strength before the person surrenders to the reality that she will not get better and may die soon. However, there also is another reality to keep in mind: There are instances when people go into remission or recover totally. So we prepare for both—life and death.

The ambiguity of holding the prospect of death in one hand and the hope of life in the other can be stressful. It is a unique situation that people not in this position have difficulty under-standing. So your best recourse is to stay centered in the middle, which is the place of being okay with not knowing. Prepare for life and for death, and trust that when the time comes to sur-render to death, your deepest wisdom will come forward to guide you.

Feeling disconnected from other people at a critical time not only is disheartening; it causes us great distress. As Jane put it to me, "The experience of giving and receiving love becomes a mere concept, so all I can trust is my intellectual knowledge." But she was blind to the behavior that pushed her children and others away. Her family resented her extreme and angry de-mands for attention "because I won't be around much longer." They felt that in her selfishness she completely ignored their needs to attend to their jobs, relationships, and lives, and so they withdrew.

The world of a person fighting for life is different from that of a healthy person. It is important for family and friends to understand something of the ill person's world, and vice versa. But no one can understand the other side completely. The focus and purpose of those on each side is different, and with the emo-tional charge that affects a family with a person who has an in-creasingly debilitating or terminal illness, it's challenging to see to everyone's needs. Also know that sometimes friends with-draw from a person with a serious illness because they fear their own mortality, or because they don't know how to act or what to say.

This is the time for honesty all around, a time for open com-munication. Then you can work out a balance of fulfilling everyone's needs. You won't worry about "pulling" on others. I

saw a dramatic shift in one extremely shy client when he began
to speak up to his overbearing mother, who wanted to smother
him with care. I had him rehearse in front of a mirror what he
wanted to tell her. "I love you, Mom," he said one day, "but you
need to quit sacrificing your life for me. I'm a grown man who
can deal with my cancer. I'll keep you up to date and ask for
help when I need it. But it's time for you to trust that I'm capable." The mother broke down crying, and was grateful for what
her son had shared. She needed only a reminder from time to
time about his ability to direct his own health care.

There are many programs at hospitals and wellness centers
that hold groups for people with cancer and other chronic and
terminal illnesses. You may find that this is the place where you
can find understanding from people who are going through the
same thing you are. And of course, you can ask for help from a
therapist, spiritual adviser, or hospice counselor.

Seemingly simple work can be very powerful. Although Jane
was not willing to practice meditation or journal writing, which
would have helped her reconnect with herself, we continued to
work on repairing her relationship with her son Seth. And she
finally "came out" at work about having cancer by not wearing
her wig, shaving her head, and walking the halls of the clinic
unadorned. This new openness allowed her coworkers to express
the concern and the support they'd been holding back, which
helped Jane to feel less lonely and depressed. Approaching death,
she was finally learning to live the life she really wanted. Here is
a practice I suggest for my clients to begin to reconnect with
family and friends. It creates a template for social connection,
and eases the possible discomfort of opening to others when one
has been emotionally isolated for a period of time.

Exercise: Staying Connected to Others

1. Sit or lie comfortably in a place where you won't be disturbed. Close your eyes. Relax your body, and take seven deep belly breaths that you let out slowly.

2. Recall a time when you and the person you wish to reconnect with had a satisfying conversation. See that person in front of you—picture the both of you engaging each other with eye contact and a feeling of positive energy.

3. In this scene, begin to share with this person. Tell him about your challenges in managing your illness, and how you haven't had time to attend to relationships. Say that you'd like to have him be a part of your life again. Imagine how the conversation might continue in a positive way.

4. Write what you experienced in your journal.

5. Repeat with two or three people with whom you wish to reconnect.

6. Phone or e-mail each person you have worked with in this exercise and initiate a connection. If you both want to stay connected, decide how that will happen.

Learn to let go

Jane also had a constricted energy about her, as if she were fighting to contain all the emotions brought up by her unrelenting depression, sense of regret, loneliness, and, toward the end, physical pain. I could tell it required tremendous effort to maintain her stance of being in control.

For those of us who are self-sufficient, hardworking, and used to being "on top of things," the experience of illness can subject us to a vulnerability we have never been forced to acknowledge before. Our strength can make us reluctant to let go of our old ways of coping and engage with the tools we need for healing and wholeness. How many times in our lives do we tell ourselves, "I don't have time"? In a moment such as this, when the time you have is literally limited, it's crucial that you drop your defenses and be willing to let go—of the paperwork on your desk, the mess in the fridge, or whatever it is you think you must attend to first.

Honor yourself

The nearness of death demands that we care for ourselves in a way we never have before.

This is our time for healing, rebalancing, and honoring ourselves. I often ask my clients who are at the end of life, "How do you experience death approaching you—slowly in a wheelchair, or speeding on a motorcycle?" Their responses are a surprisingly accurate indication of how much time they have left. If a person's answer is "motorcycle," we go deeply into an exploration of how she will honor herself. It may be the only work we do.

One way to honor yourself is by intending to *be* your true self. This means dropping artifice, giving up trying to live for others, and striving to live your truth. Here is a folktale from the Orkney Islands, at the northern tip of Scotland, that illustrates our deep longing to be our authentic self.

One day a fisherman walked by a flat rock near the ocean shore. Bathing in the sun on this rock were several Selkies, or seal-folk. Others were jumping and playing in the clear water. The fisherman admired their naked snow-white bodies, which were quite human, and their enchanted sealskins, which were discarded in a heap nearby. The fisherman crept closer to the rock and, with one swift move, snatched a skin and headed off for home. When he looked back, all the Selkies, except one beautiful woman, had donned their skins and transformed into seals swimming in the sea.

The woman followed the fisherman home, sobbing and wailing for her skin to be returned. She fell to her knees and begged for mercy, for she could not live with her own people without her skin. But the man kept walking, all the way to his hut. Finally, she offered to marry him, and he acquiesced. She was thrifty and kind, and bore the fisherman seven children. But each day she grieved for her lost life with her kin in the sea. She searched the cottage daily, but could not find where her husband had hidden her skin.

One day, one of her children asked her what she was looking for, and absentmindedly, she answered, "My skin." The child said, "Oh, you mean the one

Father keeps in this basket on top of the cupboard?"
With that, the Selkie wife grabbed her skin and ran
back to the sea. She joyfully donned her sealskin and
dived into the water, announcing to her kin that she
was her true self once again.

We can only stray from our essential self for a while, until we
become uncomfortable and yearn to return to our natural way
of being. This is especially true when we are ill or facing death.
Intending to live your truth and changing your behavior to reflect who you really are honors you, and is a primary step in
moving toward wholeness.

Often our most powerful instinct when confronted with a
difficult situation is to throw ourselves somewhere else completely, to escape in any way we can. For Jane, this escape was
work, an addiction as powerful as what other people experience
with drugs or alcohol.

She was unhappily trapped in bitter feelings about her life—
wanting more time and attention from her children, wanting a
love relationship with a partner. Really, she longed for any kind
of intimacy. But rather than addressing this longing directly by
seeking healthy ways to fulfill her desires, she buried herself in
work to the point of exhaustion. She ignored her need for rest
and play. Jane had always neglected her own inner growth, dis-
missing her dreams, creative impulses, and imagination. This is
something we often do in order to get by, to survive, and to pay
the bills.

The fact that her work was beneficial to others pulled her
even further into the daily operations of her clinic. It is often
most difficult to see our own self-neglect when the work we

perform is a service to others, as we experience the joy of knowing we help our fellow beings. However, this kind of noble service is not a substitute for self-care or self-awareness, two things we need very much indeed when we are ill. Those of us who are natural caretakers of others may find we aren't the best caretakers of ourselves, and we may be unfamiliar with our own needs and desires, as well as with how to ask for help.

Open to vulnerability

Vulnerability means openness, not weakness. Granted, we don't want to go through life emotionally wide open to everyone and everything, but with awareness, we can sense when it's appropriate and meaningful to open ourselves to life, taking down our protective barriers.

In Jane's struggles to understand her life and her illness, we've seen some of the challenges a dying person faces. With so many obstacles to overcome, the idea of peace or wholeness at life's end can seem very far away. She wanted the company of her children most of all, and if she had her way, they would still live with her and take care of her. But her strong demands for them to be present just pushed them further away. She could not be vulnerable with her children, and they couldn't trust being emotionally vulnerable with her.

I arranged a Skype meeting with her youngest son, Seth, so they could talk about what wasn't working in their relationship. They had further discussions on the phone to address what each needed to change in their relationship. Finally, Seth felt that they had made enough progress for him to visit in person.

Though their first visit went well and they became closer, as he was ready to leave, she began demanding that he come back the next week. This made him withdraw, and it was a long time before he contacted his mother again. It would have been quite a different scenario had she shared her fears of being alone and dying alone. Again, I have found that reconnection with lost parts of ourselves and with others we long to be with requires open communication and a willingness to risk being vulnerable.

Here's an exercise I offered Jane to help her connect to her relationship needs and examine how she could communicate those needs to her family. Doing this exercise will help you learn more about your current relationships with those in your life and decide if you would like to change anything. Once you begin the process of self-inquiry, it opens you to a flow of insight and further inquiry. Take your time and let your pen fill up the pages; the more you write, the more you'll learn! Be completely honest.

Exercise: Open Your Communication

Close your eyes and ask yourself these questions. Then write your responses in your journal.

1. Why is it so hard to open up? What are my feelings?

2. What do I need from my family, friends, and health care team? Be specific about what you need from each person. Write all the details about each person. Write down a clear way of communicating this

without making demands. How can I express appreciation also?

3. What is my fear behind expressing these feelings and needs?

Navigate the sea of depression, fear, and anger

Identifying our needs and being able to ask for help are especially important, because the struggles of a dying person can cause or heighten anxiety and depression. Almost everyone I've worked with experiences one of these conditions when faced with death. Fear can be seen as extreme anxiety. Having these symptoms when confronted with one's mortality is normal. Illness often exacerbates any existing struggle—what was already difficult becomes yet more so.

Despite intensive treatment with a psychiatrist and trying various medications to help with her depression, Jane remained severely depressed, and she told me, "At stage four cancer, even if I don't get a miracle healing, I want to find meaning in my life and eliminate the depression. Then dying, if that's my lot, will be more acceptable." This was a glimmer of hope, because Jane could see another way to die with some peace about her life, but her journey would not be easy.

Depression is difficult for everyone, but for someone who is fighting for his or her life, depression is like being held underwater by a gargantuan sea dragon with no possibility of escape. For some, the depression brings such despair that suicide seems to be the only way out. Anxiety and fear disrupt our lives in a similar fashion. One feels separated from the fullness of the senses, and thoughts and feelings are muffled. Or you may feel irritated at everyone around you, or obsessively worried without a logical reason. If you can't sleep, have lost your appetite and energy, are continually sad, and think about death continually, you probably are depressed. You should be honest with your physicians and spiritual advisers about these feelings.

Another sign of depression is experiencing no feeling at all or feeling disconnected from people and life. If you are losing interest in your job and activities or are having a general sense of "flatness" about your life, it's time to make some changes. Exercise, deep breathing, spending time in nature, and doing things that have had meaning for you in the past can help. But studies show that those who seek professional guidance have a better chance of lifting out of depression than those who don't.

Agitation or feeling panicked are signals pointing to anxiety disorders. Fear is very direct and it's usually easier to recognize. Sometimes medication or treatments are the cause of anxiety, fear, and depression, so be sure to talk with your physician about it—an adjustment in medication may help. Often counseling and/or medication will alleviate these symptoms, minimize pain, and in some cases even help move your illness into remission. Also, the meditation and breathing exercises found throughout this book often alleviate or eliminate these symptoms. Such was the case with an elderly client of mine, Patrick.

Patrick was anxious about everything—the people walking on the sidewalk in front of his home, who might be dangerous; water from his tap, which might kill him with chemicals when he showered; and above all, the medicine he needed to take for his kidney disease. He had been told that he had less than a year to live, so he became anxious and hypervigilant about everything. Interestingly enough, he was not suspicious of the deep breathing exercises I taught him. After practicing them several times a day, he reported that his anxiety was no longer crippling him.

Another very natural response to being diagnosed with a terminal illness is to become angry. In addition to being depressed, Jane was angry. She was angry at her doctors, coworkers, family, men, God, and life in general, and she projected her misery and fear out into the world. She had entered the dark part of the forest. This is not uncommon with ill people, and can be a natural part of any stage of terminal illness. Some statistics claim a higher survival rate for people with cancer who are able to get angry, but I'm not convinced that's true. Yes, anger activates an engagement with life, but it also can stress the immune system. A harmonious flow in the bodymind system equally fosters healing. It's the ill person who is completely passive who has the lowest chance of survival.

Anger can be productive when it arises out of a newfound connection with one's own feelings and responses to the dying process, and when we are able to move past it by opening into vulnerability. The day Jane finally got angry with me during one of our sessions was also the day she finally wept as she faced her fear of dying.

Anger happens when we feel we are losing something of value. It is a protective defense against that loss. People with illness, and terminal illness especially, are losing control of their lives in many ways. The illness creates a series of violations against one's chosen life. Our freedom of choice is narrowed considerably or lost with the need for medical treatments. In many cases our relationships change instantly with the announcement of terminal illness—we may be treated like a child or avoided altogether, and the grieving may start. People are careful with their speech when we are around. They whisper, or hold back their communication. This is difficult for most of us, and of course it too can cause feelings of anger.

If you are a person who is not used to experiencing anger, the strong feelings can be confusing. Sometimes your anger may be so strong that it explodes on family and friends. Sometimes it comes out with nurses and doctors. You may be angry at God.

Know that your anger is righteous and normal—but consider that you may really be angry at your disease. You're not truly angry at the people who don't have a pronouncement of death hanging over them. You are angry at the disease that is threatening your life, the thing that you value the most. There are other losses that can make you angry—you may never be married, or have a child, or be able to achieve your goals, etc. It feels like everything you value is being stripped away. When you direct your anger toward the injustice of having a terminal disease and the losses and violations it creates instead of toward the people you love, your suffering is lessened and the anger becomes manageable or even goes away.

The first step to freeing yourself from depression, fear, or anxiety is to get to know it. The paradox is that we need to go into our experience of these emotions and recognize our own particular triggers for them before we can lessen their strength or frequency. So put on your detective hat and make an honest assessment. Take some time to reflect and write in your journal:

Exercise: Assess Your Emotional Life

1. How often do I feel angry, depressed, fearful, or anxious? How does each show up? How long do they last? What helps get me out of these emotions? How do they limit me? What do I need when they happen? What are my thoughts about this? Write all the details. Give examples.

2. What and how will I share this with my physicians, my spiritual advisers, and the people closest to me?

Once we have identified the triggers and causes of difficult emotions, we can begin to shift the energies of fear, anxiety, irritability, or depression so they have a chance to dissipate. The following breathing meditation changes our physiology into a relaxed state. Whenever we quiet our bodies, we also relax our minds, and vice versa. Working with our breath is one of the quickest and most effective ways to release ourselves from the grip of difficult emotions. Letting our breathing quiet down and focusing on our natural breathing cycle clears difficult emotions and clutter from our minds. We become aware of where we are uncomfortable in our bodies, and we connect with deeper feelings of peacefulness. No matter how disturbed we may feel, underneath those emotions is a deep well of peace and contentment. With practice, we can easily drink from this well. Healing and a sense of well-being happen when our bodyminds are in a relaxed state.

Bodymind is a term that recognizes our minds and bodies as one unified organism rather than two separate entities; when there is a disturbance or enhancement in one part of the system, the whole organism is affected.

One of the quickest ways to shift our emotional energy is to focus on our breathing.

The following meditation is used in many traditions and known by many names. Here, we'll call it:

Exercise: Belly Breath Meditation

1. Find a quiet place. Sit in a relaxed position and put your hand on your belly. Place all your attention on the rising and falling of your lower belly as you breathe naturally.

2. Relax your jaw and your shoulders. Just notice the sensation of your belly rising and falling, without analyzing it. If thoughts arise, release them, and gently bring your attention back to your breathing. Focus on the motion of your belly going up and down in rhythm with your breath.

3. Do this for five minutes in the morning, and again in the afternoon.

No matter how much time you have left on earth, you deserve to spend it feeling more like your normal self. As soon as you are aware of a difficult emotion beginning to arise, stop what you are doing and go to a quiet place where you can sit quietly and do some deep breathing, or the Belly Breath Meditation. The more quickly you can halt the progression of overwhelming emotions, the better your chance of lessening or eliminating them.

Shift to new ways of being

A wise teacher of transformation, Brugh Joy, often said, "You can't heal the problem at the level of the problem." When we are immersed in the challenges of illness and the prospect of death, we often feel stuck in a morass of problems, with no apparent way out. It's important to lift ourselves out of that morass, just as Jane did.

Even though Jane had just completed another round of chemo, she wanted to accompany me on a group trip I was leading to Bali. My coleader, William Coke Harrell, MD, agreed to supervise her medical regime as we traveled. The trip was good for her, and it also brought her closer to her fear of death. The Balinese have complex beliefs and rituals about death. An entire village participates in a colorful, noisy procession to the place where the body is cremated. A priest rides the pallet carrying the corpse, shouting and praying loudly to keep evil spirits from entering the deceased's body. They believe that the deceased interact with the living and are still an integral part of the community. Everyone witnesses the cremation, grieving and celebrating at the same time. It is very dramatic. Jane was deeply affected when she witnessed the burning body atop the pile of wood, realizing that the end of her physical life was very real.

The trip helped Jane get "unstuck." She learned to value meditation and devotional ceremonies, and found a connection to the web of all life. She felt less lonely.

Sometimes we become so tightly adhered to our beliefs,

surroundings, and routine that we forget there are other ways of seeing and being. "Inner travel" and visualization can be entry points to transformation. Of course, we might choose to literally go somewhere as Jane did, but we also can accomplish these kinds of shifts through visualization, meditation, and imagery, as in the following exercise.

Exercise: Find Your Healing Place

1. Close your eyes and take four deep belly breaths.

2. Imagine a peaceful place in nature where you would like to be.

3. Place yourself there. Use your imagination to see, feel, hear, and experience everything around you. Include lots of details about your surroundings. Feel your body-mind doing what it wants to do in this environment. Stay here as long as you wish, relaxing more and more.

4. Petition the Healing Presence to join you now—a sacred figure or the vital energy of all life. Envision it sweeping through your bodymind and soul, healing and transforming.

5. Open your eyes and come back to the present. Keep the peaceful feeling you experienced. You can come back to your healing place, even for a few minutes, as often as you wish.

6. In your journal, write about your healing place and what you experienced. Describe images, feelings, thoughts, and insights.

In this chapter you have learned to engage with your life by honoring yourself, dealing with difficult emotions, healing your relationships, and shifting to new ways of being. When you address these areas of your life, you are creating a foundation for transformation and moving toward wholeness.

CHAPTER 2

Practice Energy Medicine

Without energy, there is death. The world is run
by energy, and so is our human body.

—Unknown teacher of Chinese medicine

The practice of working with human energy fields is known
by many names—energy medicine, pranic healing, bioenergy therapy, and energy healing or clearing, among others. It's
found in some form in every tribal culture and civilization, and
it is based on the idea that there is an infinite energy field interpenetrating the earth and the universe, which is the fundamental substance of all life, all creation. This field of energy
surrounds and permeates our sun, the planets and stars, and
space itself. It is our human vital energy as well, suffusing every
nerve, cell, tissue, organ, bone, and fluid in our bodies. Our
consciousness is a part of this primordial energy field also. *It connects every being, object, and event in existence.*

Mystical teachings from ancient spiritual traditions reveal that
we, as humans, have the right to harness this universal energy for
healing, creativity, and manifestation. Since our consciousness is
a part of this unified energy field, if we focus our attention on the
desired flow of energy to a place in the body, energy will easily go
there, infusing that area with new life. Theoretically, new tissue
can replace damaged cells and the healing process will occur more

speedily than usual. An energy treatment also can wash away mental anxieties and disruptive thought patterns. Does this sound too magical to be true? Even though concrete healing results of energy medicine are not easily proven by scientific method, I do observe these benefits occurring in my clients. Of course, not everyone experiences a "miracle" healing from energy work, but I have seen it happen. Whether or not these results are due to the placebo effect is irrelevant; if clients find energy medicine valuable—and most do—I use it.

One of my favorite depictions of energy healing is found on ancient Egyptian pottery: people standing around a table, extending their hands over a person lying there, manipulating the energy field for healing and balance. In Chinese medicine this intrinsic life energy is called "chi" or "qi." Many consider qigong to be the father of all energy medicine. Interaction with energy fields also is at the center of martial arts like tai chi, and movement of energy in the body is an intrinsic part of yoga practice and philosophy in the Hindu traditions. For a further explanation of the human energy field, which includes chakras—energy centers in the human field—and its other aspects, see the resources listed at the end of this book.

During the past forty years there has been exponential growth in the study of human energy fields, both in science and in the healing arts. Some are rigorous, evidence-based studies, and others are based upon anecdotal claims. The notion that we humans, as well as all living organisms, are encased and permeated by a bioelectrical field that can be harnessed as a healing agent is not accepted by most scientists. And to date, the bulk of experiments trying to measure and prove that human energy fields (auras) extend several feet beyond our bodies have been inconclusive or nonreplicable by rigorous scientific standards. Perhaps this is because we haven't yet developed instruments that are able to reliably detect and measure the human energy field. Nonetheless, pioneering teachers in medical schools and increased public interest have brought energy medicine into the mainstream of the healing arts. There is a corresponding development in the field of energy psychology, with therapies such as EMDR (eye movement desensitization and reprocessing), Emotional Freedom Technique, and Thought Field Therapy, among others.

Most physicians today are amenable to their patients receiving acupuncture, Reiki, energy work, spiritual energy healing, or any of the myriad alternative methods of energy balancing along with conventional medical treatment. Albert Szent-Györgyi, who received the Nobel Prize in Physiology or Medicine in 1937, emphasized that in every culture and medical tradition before modern times, healing was effected by moving energy.

The reason energy work has entered the mainstream is that no matter what we believe about it, anecdotal experience has shown that people benefit from receiving it. Whether it's spiritual energy, a balancing of the chakras, or merely a relaxation response ultimately doesn't matter—people report that they feel better or even that their symptoms are healed. It's how they feel afterward that counts. I've had clients report everything ranging from pain elimination to symptoms disappearing, radical healings, or a positive mood change after a treatment. Even those who say they didn't feel energy moving during an energy balancing want to do it again because they felt it was a positive experience. And everyone enjoys the deep relaxation they feel after a treatment.

So I invite you to practice the following energy balancing exercises to experiment for yourself. While the second exercise involves giving and sharing of energy with another or others, the first is one you can do alone at any time. Although there are more intricate systems of techniques for working with energy medicine or healing, you could practice just these two for a lifetime and intuitively learn everything you need to know. *Practice* is the key word—for most it takes a few times to develop the sensitivity to perceive energy flow. Your intention, or purpose for doing this, should be clear in your mind. And you will learn to hold your attention on the flow of energy through your body with practice. Wherever you place your attention, energy flows there. A recurring principle in esoteric texts is "energy follows thought."

You may do the following exercise anytime you wish. Find a quiet time and place, and decide if you want to play some meditative music or do the session in silence. Sometimes you'll cycle through the steps very slowly and will want to stay in the energy for as long as an hour, and at others you'll feel complete after ten or fifteen minutes. Follow your intuition.

Exercise: Energy Self-Balancing

1. Form an intention for your energy session. Do you want to balance your whole body and mind? Heal a major disease? Eliminate tension or fatigue? Accelerate healing of an injury? Get rid of a cold? Have more mental focus? State this to yourself as you sit comfortably in a chair with your feet on the ground.

2. Close your eyes. Relax your shoulders, jaw, and belly. Take seven deep breaths from your lower abdomen, exhaling as slowly as you can. Then breathe normally.

3. Envision the Creator, Mother Nature, the Source of all life, Universal Mind, or your own image of the transcendent. Know that you are able to connect to this source.

4. Visualize light emanating from the source and touching the crown of your head, where it gathers into a spinning ball of light energy. It is pristine, beautiful light. It is abundant and ever flowing. Keep your attention on the ball of light for a few minutes. Take your time. You will probably feel a tingling or warmth, or slight pressure on your scalp. If thoughts enter your mind, bring your attention back to the spinning light on your crown.

5. Using your imagination, let the light easily flow down. The energy will both pass through your head and surround it with a gentle and powerful light. You may feel a vibration in your eyes as the energy pulsates. Know that the energy has intelligence and knows what to do. It's balancing, healing, enlivening—every cell, tissue, bone, and fluid. Let go and enjoy the feeling.

6. When you are ready, see the energy flowing to your throat, inside and outside. It flows as easily as water down a hill. Give it time to do its work. You will know how long to keep your attention here. After a few minutes you will be ready to shift to the next area.

7. Continue moving the energy down to your heart chakra, the energy center between your breasts. Feel

a ball of light energy in your heart, spinning and enlarg-
ing. It fills your whole chest, inside and out, front and
back. Hold your awareness at your heart and feel the
pulsations and warmth. Let go even more. Stay with
the light in your heart for as long as you wish. Your
heart is the center of unconditional love.

8. Let the energy flow to fill your whole trunk: your
chest, your upper and lower abdomen, and your pel-
vic area. The light expands to fill your body and swirls
around it. It flows through your arms and hands. The
energy swirls easily and fully in its own way—you
don't need to force it. Relax into the feeling of this
nourishing light. Feel the energy in your back and but-
tocks. Your whole body may feel tingly or warm. You
may feel a bit sleepy. Know that the energy is healing
and transforming every cell, tissue, organ, bone, and
fluid in your body.

9. See and feel the energy continuing to flow down
through and around your legs to your feet. Let them
soak up the light energy.

10. Direct the energy to any part of your body that needs
special attention for pain relief or healing. Keep your
awareness there for a while.

11. Sense your body from head to toe, as the energy
washes through in a steady stream. Know that toxins
and energies that are no longer needed are being
washed away, eliminated through your feet into the
earth for recycling. Consciously think, "I release
_____ from my body, and _____ from my
mind." Take your time. Enjoy the flow of energy from
top to toe.

12. When you are ready, place both hands over your heart center. Allow yourself to feel gratitude for your experience. Stay with your heart energy for a moment. Open your eyes and notice your surroundings. Make sure you are grounded and alert before moving around.

If you are new to energy work, you may want to record in your journal what sensations you felt in your body and in your mind after doing this exercise. Perhaps you felt tingling, or heat, or pressure in your body. Or you may experience a relief from tension somewhere, or a "freeing" sensation in your mind. Some experience joy, or a sense of peace. Whatever your experience, notice if you feel different than before your treatment.

A few weeks after our Bali trip, Jane—from the previous chapter—began to have pain in her abdomen and dizziness from the pain medication, and she felt tired all the time. She couldn't go to work, and her depression increased. Because she wasn't able to drive to my office for our sessions, I went to her home. It took her a long time to drag herself to the door. We sat in her living room, where she wrapped herself in blankets and talked in a slow, small voice. "This is it," she said. "I don't have any hope at all. I hate feeling so sluggish. I can't think straight."

"When is your next scan?" I asked.

"Next Tuesday. I don't know why they bother—it's just getting worse."

It seemed like the right time to ask Jane again if she wanted to explore energy medicine; I hoped she'd be open to it. I had tried before, but to no avail. This time she assented, and when I channeled the unconditional love of universal healing energy into her, she received it like a dried-up sponge takes in water.

Jane's shift to a compassionate, loving person occurred in the last stage of her illness. All the work we had done was helpful, I believe. But it was when she finally gave herself permission to open to the practice of energy medicine that she made a noticeable transformation. While she reluctantly began the practice of balancing her own energy field, she soon looked forward to her self-balancing twice a day. She felt less pain and her mood improved. Her positive experiences with me in receiving and giving energy lifted her from a limited, guarded view of herself and the world into an expansive awareness that was transcendent. With the shift of attitude that came from this experience, she was able to relate to her family and others in an open, loving way. Before her death she attained a state of peace and love for the first time in her life.

How do I die?

The kind of energy-balancing work described in the previous section brought Jane great peace. But she received more bad news after her next visit to the oncologist. The cancer had spread even further, into her liver. Jane told me she was afraid that in dying she would somehow "screw it up." This is a common fear. In fact, though, there's nothing to screw up. Dying is a natural process, and you know automatically how to do it. Our souls knew how to get born into the world, and they have the wisdom and skill to leave it. We will be guided all the way, and all we need to do is let go when the time comes. Surrender to it—which is *not* the same thing as giving up. It might even be a great adventure. She told me more about her beliefs of having spirit guides and teachers, and that she hoped they would accompany her when it was her time to go. Jane was wide open and vulnerable during those last visits. Her defenses had crumbled.

I knew she would die soon. Jane let me call her children. All three arrived a few days later. They had a chance to share their true feelings of love and gratitude for one another. Then, she asked if they would join her in sharing energy with each other. We went into the bedroom, where Jane lay on the bed. She was the first in the family to receive a balancing as I instructed her children how to share energy with one another. As she lay on the bed and felt the energy from her children, tears rolled down her cheeks. "I'm so happy," she said.

One person can give energy to another, or in this case, there were four of us sharing energy with Jane at the same time. It was a beautiful experience. Here is the exercise I taught them that day.

Exercise: Sharing Energy

You may share energy anytime you are undisturbed in a quiet place. I like to receive a treatment at the end of the day and then go off to sleep. Both you and the recipient of your offering probably will experience tension leaving your body, a quieter mind, and a deep feeling of relaxation and peace. Both parties involved enter a coherent healing flow, where there is no separation. Hopefully, any pain or discomfort will be ameliorated. Many people feel a radical sense of renewal.

1. Have a friend or partner lie down in front of you on a bed, the floor, or a massage table with their eyes closed. Ask what part of the body needs attention for pain relief or healing. Inquire about mental tensions he or she wants to release. You may put on some quiet music if desired, or do the session in silence.

2. Connect to your source and let the light energy flow into your crown, head, neck, and then your heart. Enjoy the feeling of opening to unconditional love as you feel the energy spinning in your heart.

3. After you have activated your heart center, visualize the energy flowing down your arms to your hands, where the light forms energy balls that cover each hand. You will probably feel your hands heat up or tingle. Place all your attention on the flow of light from head to heart to hands.

4. Open your mind and heart even more to the feeling of unconditional love, a love that accepts and appreciates another totally and gives without any strings attached.

5. Place the palms of your hands lightly on an area of your partner's body that needs attention for pain relief or healing. Concentrate on the flow of energy from the source down to your heart, through your hands, into the body of your partner. Hold your hands steady on the area. The energy concentrates here, and flows through the whole body. You will sense when this area has received enough energy. This is your cue that it's time to move your hands to another place.

6. Use your intuition to place your hands lightly on other areas of your partner's body that you sense need attention. Or you may want to do a whole-body

balancing from head to toe. Take your time and enjoy the experience. There is no right or wrong.

7. You will sense when it's time to finish. Starting at your partner's feet, place your hands a few inches above the body and brush the air upward toward the head. You are smoothing and sealing your partner's energy field.

8. Sit quietly for a few minutes, feeling gratitude for the opportunity to share energy with another. Then gently tap your partner's hand to signal that you are finished.

9. Consciously disconnect your field from your partner's. Visualize yourself in a vibrating egg of light that is separate from your partner's energy field. Think to yourself that you are now separating your field from his or hers. You have been bonded in an intimate way, and it is important to assert that you are once again separate individuals.

10. Your partner may want to talk about the experience. You also may want to share what you noticed and felt.

11. Make sure you both feel grounded before you move on to other activities. If anyone is shaky or drowsy, drinking water or eating a piece of fruit can be helpful.

Energy medicine can be very powerful. Sometimes people receiving the treatment cry or have an emotional release with lots of sighing, deep feelings, or even laughter. They can report experiences of seeing light or feeling strong electrical currents in their bodies. Sometimes their muscles twitch, or movement or heat occurs in various body parts. Often they have thoughts or dreamlike experiences that prove to be valuable insights. Or, some people just lie quietly on the table, feeling relaxed—which is worth a lot. Know that whatever happens is right for that person. Your job is to deliver the energy from a centered, heart-felt place; don't be attached to what your partner experiences.

It's tempting to think that a more dramatic experience indicates more significant results, but that's not true. One client I remember, Ivan, was very disappointed when he felt that "nothing happened" when I taught him the self-balancing exercise. But fifteen minutes after he left my office, Ivan pounded on my door and excitedly told me that his ankle no longer hurt, which had constantly been painful since he had broken it two years earlier. I have lots of stories about my family members, friends, and clients who have benefited from energy medicine, and I've also seen positive results from shamanic energy work in the tribal societies I've visited. The path of energy medicine is an amazing exploration.

~

It is never too late for transformation. It can happen even during the last minutes of life. In her final days, Jane felt connected to life for the first time since childhood. She was joyful. She explained to her children and me that she was ready to go. I shared a favorite quote by Pablo Neruda with her: "In the end, everyone is aware of this: Nobody keeps any of what he has, and life is only a borrowing of bones."

She told us, "I want to be cremated. I want you to scatter my ashes under a grove of trees on the side of a mountain, so they can sink into this beautiful earth and nourish it. Some part of me will be here forever." We told her she would be with us always in our hearts.

Hospice service came the next day, reliable as always, bringing a hospital bed, medical equipment, oxygen, and medication, setting up the bed in the living room. Their job is to make a person's transition comfortable and carry out the physician's orders. Each nurse who had a shift the next three days was comforting and attended to Jane with care and compassion. They were there around the clock.

When I arrived for my last visit, all three of her children were in the den playing cards and eating pizza, acting as if it were a casual weekend family gathering. Long ago I had gotten used to the strange scenarios of the deathbed watch. Families can grieve only so much, until storytelling, watching TV, practical discussion of who gets what, and bad jokes arise. And then another cycle of grieving or weepy personal expression occurs. It's all very human and natural, and it's important not to judge.

"She asked for you this morning," her son, Seth, said. "I think she's in a coma or something now, 'cause she can't speak anymore. None of us wants to be there when she dies—we just can't. The nurse says it'll be about a week more," he added. He took me to her bed and he and the nurse went to the kitchen.

As I approached her, I could tell she was frightened. Her eyes were wide open, she was trembling slightly, and her breath was shallow and labored. I felt she was pleading for help. I opened my heart and flooded her with unconditional love. I talked to her and stroked her forehead, telling her that everything was going to be okay and she could let go whenever she was ready. I assured her that her children would be fine, that she had raised them well and everything she had taught them was in place, and that I would check in with them after she was gone. I thanked her for our years together, saying she had added to my life and I would miss her. When I took my hand away from her forehead, she whimpered and seemed distressed, so I put it back and continued stroking and talking close to her ear.

"All you need to do is let go when you're ready; just let go. Your soul knows what to do, so you can relax. Everything is prepared."

I sensed the familiar intensification of energy around her, a subtle perturbation in the air that precedes death in those I've been with at the final moment. We were touched by the sacred that is beyond understanding. My intuition always provides words at this time and I said, "They're here for you, Jane."

In a minute she was gone.

Although it had taken several years of self-exploration and working with her dreams, habitual self-destructive thoughts, and energy medicine, Jane finally experienced her own wholeness. She felt connected to her children and sensed that she was at one with spirit. She appreciated the challenges life had brought her, and finally learned to love herself.

Each person's path toward wholeness is unique, and when we take the first step, the way unfolds to guide us.

CHAPTER 3

Examine Your Beliefs

In death, I am born.   —Hopi proverb

Our belief systems strongly motivate us in everything we do. The problem is that these beliefs become such a central part of who we are that often we operate from them automatically, eliminating any chance of a fresh perspective that might be helpful. Initially, our beliefs are inherited from our parents without question, and somewhere during the late teens or early adulthood when we encounter different beliefs, we begin to think for ourselves and perhaps make other choices about what is true or valuable. This becomes a rich time of solidifying values, and sometimes creates conflict within the family.

At no time other than during terminal or increasingly debilitating illness do we more squarely wrestle with our belief systems. We have beliefs about which type of medical support is best—homeopathic, allopathic, chiropractic, oriental medicine, etc., or no treatment at all. We have beliefs about the role of spiritual practices for the end of life; they could be a core value or seen as unnecessary. We may believe we have a role in creating the illness, or believe it is an entirely random occurrence. We hold beliefs about what the best conditions to exit this world are and how that should happen. One of the biggest influences on how we die is whether or not we believe in an afterlife. All of these beliefs come to the forefront as we face the prospect of death.

Being seriously ill within a caring family sometimes initiates an even stronger clash of values when we are confronted with the beliefs of the people around us. Often family or friends, out of their best intentions, push their belief systems on the person who is ill. They may insist on acupuncture—which they believe can cure everything—or demand an experimental surgery because they believe modern medicine is the only way to go, even during the stage when the ill person is ready to complete his or her life. Often a person in end-stage illness must deal with a barrage of suggested remedies that friends believe will help, and spend precious energy worrying that they have offended when they decline to try them.

We also encounter the belief systems of the health care personnel attending to us. A physician who does not believe in the usefulness of complementary or alternative treatment modes can make the patient who wants to try those methods feel foolish. I have seen people give up their beliefs and preferences just to keep the peace. Ideally, the family, friends, and health care team will support the dying person's core beliefs and choices.

Why am I ill?

When we are faced with a life-limiting illness, we naturally want to know "why me?" It never feels fair. We know we are good people who have contributed to others. We may have taken really good care of ourselves—exercised and eaten healthy food. Some people feel guilty for getting sick or even believe any circumstance we encounter is something we've brought on ourselves. One example I've often heard to illustrate this notion is the belief that knee problems are created when a person isn't humble enough, when he or she hasn't metaphorically knelt down. Similarly, breast cancer is said to be created when a woman doesn't nourish herself or others enough, or conversely, when she is the mother type who controls others through over-giving. Within this line of thought, physical healing cannot happen until the inner problem is resolved. Sometimes this idea stems from a belief in karma, misinterpreted as a cosmic system of punishment administered through illness or tragedy for misdeeds in this or past lives.

While we certainly *participate* in the creation of illness through lifestyle choices and unconscious processes, complex factors such as environment and genetics play a major part in why we get sick. Then, of course, there is randomness, the hand of cards dealt us by an impersonal universe. We should no more blame ourselves for becoming ill than we would blame a person for being born into hardship. No one should shoulder the burden of thinking they have total responsibility for creating their illness. Of course, lifestyle and psycho-spiritual issues deserve to be examined, but give up any guilt you may have about contracting an illness. Choose to spend your time and energy engaging with your life in positive ways, instead of ruminating in guilt about becoming ill, because that is antithetical to wholeness.

Exercise: I Believe

Because you are or will be making important choices, this exercise helps you clarify what's important to you. Knowing exactly what you believe about the last stage of illness in your life makes these choices easier.

The following exercise will help you discover details about your belief system. Get your journal and pen and find a peaceful place to sit.

1. Take seven deep breaths and let them out very slowly, while at the same time relaxing your jaw, shoulders, and belly so you feel free and open. Write your answers to the following questions.

2. Do I believe someone at my stage of illness can recover? If so, what would it take for me to recover mentally, physically, and spiritually?

3. Do I believe there is a relationship between my illness and the way I've lived my life? If so, how? After you've finished with this section, check to make sure your inner critic wasn't in charge of the writing. If so, write another response from the compassionate part of yourself.

4. What are my spiritual beliefs about the death process? Describe what you believe happens—are we met by deceased relatives or guides, etc.?

5. What do I believe about the afterworld? Do I believe in reincarnation?

6. When it is time for me to leave this earth, what do I believe is important for me or others to do, if anything? What is the environment I want around me in the days before my death? Whom do I want to be there? Describe any ceremony or actions you want those present to observe. Also clarify medical

considerations, such as instigating a "do not resuscitate" order.

7. What are my beliefs and wishes about how my body should be treated after my death?

8. Whatever your beliefs and wishes may be, discuss them now with your family and friends, no matter how difficult. Both you and they will be greatly relieved to have this conversation. Usually people are unsure how to address these issues, so when you take the courage to share them, you'll be doing yourself and them a favor and you'll be assured your beliefs and wishes will be honored.

One of my clients benefited greatly from sharing her preferences and beliefs. She struggled with her Hopi traditions when she became ill and entered the medical system.

Arica was thirty-two years old, of Native American descent; her parents moved to Phoenix from the Hopi reservation before she was born. Throughout her childhood, her family went back to the reservation during summer vacations, where she learned the traditional Hopi way of life. She felt closely tied to the land and the spiritual values her culture embraced. Ten years ago she moved to Los Angeles to study fashion design, aspiring to learn the business and create a clothing line. She was not able to complete her courses because of the expense and because of the demands of her job at a clothing factory, but it still was her dream.

Her boyfriend, Kumar, was born in India and his parents resided there. They arranged for him to live with relatives in the

United States when he was twenty so he would have "splendid opportunities." He sent them money each month, retaining a minimal amount for his own expenses. He and Arica lived together in an apartment they shared with four Hindu friends in downtown Los Angeles near the garment district, where they all worked. They planned to get married next year.

At the hospital clinic, Arica had heard from someone that I help people who are ill, and that I had spent time on the Hopi reservation. She got in touch, and at our first meeting, I told her how I had met the Hopi elder who befriended me and welcomed me into her home on the reservation, and how for many years she would join my seminars around the country and teach the Hopi way of life. During the times I took groups to the reservation and facilitated them in vision quests, Mother, as I called her, was an honored part of the ceremonies.

And when I stayed with her, she taught me to dig holes in the field with a planting stick, to plant dried corn kernels, and how to care for the plant as it grew. Many months later we harvested the fields, and cooked whole ears of corn in the fire's ashes to serve to our neighbors. Those village gatherings were magical. Such a feeling of community! She was an amazing woman, and I'm so grateful we were in each other's lives. Every time I look at the corn maiden kachina doll on my desk, I feel the energy of the vision quests, the healing ceremonies, and the kachina dances that were held in the villages. I had profound spiritual experiences when she taught me about cooperating with nature and the healing power of plants. She and her village were traditionalists, who honored the old ways and didn't accept government help. This meant they had to endure hardships like carrying buckets of water by hand for long distances because they don't have water piped into their homes. Mother has been gone several years now, and though the experiences we had together live on within me, I miss her.

Our beliefs can affect our health care

Arica told me she had cancer in her liver. It started out as hepatitis C, then turned into primary cancer. She had pain on her right side, under her ribs, and in her back. "I've started chemotherapy," she said. "They're putting it right into my liver." This meant the medication was inserted directly into her liver and would not destroy the surrounding tissues.

She became distressed as she told me her problem with the doctors. "I asked if I could smudge—brush smoke from burning sage—the medication package before they prepared it for treatment. The hospital staff said no, they couldn't have smoke in the room. It made me so mad! I can't get them to understand it'll work better if I ask the healing spirits to come and help. I believe this and know it's true. Aren't we supposed to have freedom of religion? The Bahanna—white people—don't get it. And I want to put up my prayer ties too, but they'll just shoot that down. It started in my first grade, when the teacher always called on me and the other Indian kids last, and never gave us good grades—she hated Indian kids. All the teachers did. The white kids picked on us too. I know it's prejudiced, but if I'm honest, I don't like the whites. Sorry, I didn't mean you."

Arica needed to vent her frustration. She was caught between two worlds, bravely trying to incorporate her Native

American practices into her Western medical treatment, and for her, both approaches were necessary for her recovery. Although she had been born into Western culture, during this time of stress the appeal of indigenous life gripped her strongly and gave her hope. She wanted ancient ceremony and prayer to be prominent in her healing program. When she told me that returning to her parents' home in Phoenix, close to traditional medicine people, wasn't an option because she wanted to be here with Kumar, he put his arm around her and pulled her close. "We'll get through this," he murmured. She added that she hadn't told her family about her illness, since she expected to get better and didn't want to worry them.

Share your beliefs with your health care team

I've worked with several people who didn't let their physicians know how important certain spiritual practices were for them. One woman, Nancy, was certain that if her surgical team didn't say the Lord's Prayer before they began her operation, it was bound to be a failure. She was certain the doctor was far too important and busy to even hear her request, so she kept quiet—and for weeks she was a nervous wreck. Finally, with me at her side for courage, she reached the surgeon and blurted out her concern. To her surprise, the surgeon said he would gladly carry out her request to involve the staff in the operating room—that he always said the prayer silently to himself anyway before he began. Health care personnel and hospitals know the value of spiritual beliefs, and have resources to aid their patients.

One universal spiritual belief is that meditation creates an internal home base of peace, which is a valuable healing agent during health challenges.

What is meditation?

The practice of meditation is found in all religions throughout the world, and has been a subject of scientific investigation for many years. There has been so much written about meditation recently that it can be confusing. Since Alan Watts popularized Buddhism in the Western world during the 1960s, each year produces more new meditative techniques with interesting names like Heart Math and Spherical Awareness. There is disagreement among religious and scientific circles about what elements are necessary to be able to say that a practice is indeed meditation. For simplicity, here are three qualities that are common to all meditative techniques:

1. A relaxed physical and mental state
2. An intention to shift to an altered state of awareness—one that is different from the usual, everyday state of mind
3. An expectation that meditation brings valuable results—mentally, physically, spiritually, or socially

We can describe different meditation types in this way:

1. *Concentration meditations.* We focus our attention on a phrase, repetitive prayer, sound, or object. Focusing on specific breathing patterns is the basis of many meditative techniques,

as are visualization practices. These techniques usually have specific goals. By keeping our minds in one-pointed awareness, we reduce the stress of trying to keep up with our thoughts that are jumping around like monkeys. And when our minds relax, our bodies follow their lead.

2. *Open awareness meditations.* Instead of focusing on something, we simply notice whatever comes into our awareness. We may follow sensations we feel in our bodies, noticing and feeling them, then letting them go and noticing what comes next. We might also notice what images appear in our minds spontaneously. An advanced form of open awareness meditation is to aim for a spacious awareness that has infrequent thoughts, or no thoughts at all.

3. *Movement meditations.* Included here are yoga, tai chi, and some martial arts. Others are "free movement," in which we close our eyes and move slowly and intuitively in response to quiet music. Free movement is not meant to be a choreographed dance, but an expression of our minds and bodies moving spontaneously in the moment.

4. *Spiritual meditations.* These are based on communicating with a deity or with universal forces. Their form is open and could take that of any of the preceding descriptions. We might think of a problem and listen for the solution. Or connect to spiritual energies for renewal and inspiration for others and ourselves.

Practice meditation

The key word here is *practice*, because the more we encourage ourselves to meditate, the easier it becomes and the more we reap physical, mental, and spiritual benefits. There always is a challenge to settle down and do it, but once we establish a regular habit of meditation, we enjoy it. Whether our purpose and belief involves connecting with spiritual forces or we believe meditation maximizes health and well-being, regular, daily meditation—even as little as ten minutes a day—is beneficial.

When I introduced the topic, Arica said she had never meditated—that prayers were instead used in the Hopi tradition. After this discussion Arica and Kumar were inspired to make meditation a part of their daily routine, and they reported that meditating in the evening had become a pleasure that completed their day.

At the end of our first session, Arica was happy. She said she felt filled with hope and wanted to say a prayer she had learned from her father. "I can't remember the whole thing," she said. "This is just a part:"

> Let me walk in beauty, and make my eyes behold the
> red and purple sunsets. Make my hands respect what
> you have made and sharpen my ears to hear your
> voice. Make me wise so I can understand the things
> you taught our people, and let me learn the lessons
> you've hidden in every leaf and rock.

"Om . . . om . . . om . . ." chanted Kumar as she finished. One type of meditation you can personalize to reflect your belief system is *mantra meditation*. This is a focused meditation practice that is found in all religious traditions, either sung as a chant or repeated silently or out loud.

Exercise: Mantra Meditation

In a mantra meditation, you repeat a phrase that rhythmically soothes your busy mind and circulates energy in the body. People who chant mantras report that it clears the mind and helps them focus. A mantra also may be a prayer to a deity. Experiment with saying the phrase both out loud and then silently, or you may sing it. You may do this meditation for as little as five minutes or keep it going continuously as you sit quietly or do quiet activities at home. You can create any phrase that has meaning for you, or use religious prayers.

Often, when you have worked for a time with a mantra, you can hear it in the background, even when you're not trying to say it, such as when you converse or do your work. If you're having trouble coming up with your own mantra, you may choose one from the following list and repeat it over and over, taking in the meaning of the phrase. If your attention wanders, bring it back to the mantra. Use a timer if you wish, for at least ten minutes.

1. Today I will be present in all I think, say, and do.

2. May I become kindness, generosity, wisdom, and love.

3. I open to the opportunities presented to me today.

4. Psalm 23:4. Yea, though I walk through the valley of the shadow of death, I will fear no evil: for thou art with me; thy rod and thy staff they comfort me.

5. Loving-kindness Meditation:

> May I be happy. May I be well. May I be safe.
> May I be peaceful and at ease.
>
> May you be happy. May you be well. May you
> be safe. May you be peaceful and at ease.

6. Praise Allah, who created the heavens and earth and my beautiful life. Or the shortened version: Praise Allah.

7. I embody, express, and become unconditional love.

One of my clients who had leukemia got so much relief from meditation that she believed it would cure her disease. Everyone tried to discourage her from stopping her treatments, but she insisted, believing that the energies and calm that came from meditating would be enough to heal her. Every day she meditated for an hour in the morning, an hour at noon, an hour in the early evening, and once again at bedtime. For three months she meditated with this pattern, and sometimes on weekends she would add more meditation periods. Beliefs are very strong, and amazingly, in her case she was right. After three months without treatment, her disease went into remission. I'm not recommending you stop your medication or treatment, but I want to illustrate the power of belief and consistent meditation.

Trace the origin of your beliefs

It's important to discover where your beliefs come from. Do they come from the heart of your religion? Are they based on fears? Or are they an intuitive knowing that feels right to you? Fear- or defeatist-based beliefs are limiting and keep us from moving toward wholeness. So many times I've seen people dismiss medical treatment that would help them with their chronic illness with a sweeping statement like, "Oh, that's poison—I'll never take that." Or as one person recently told me, "Everyone dies from this disease. Always. There's no use trying anything." They certainly have the right to choose no treatment at all, but a decision that originates from fear without consideration of all the facts is unwise.

One set of beliefs you may want to examine closely is your thinking about the course of your illness and how it will turn out. Rather than reinforce a belief that you will suffer greatly or not have any meaning to your life in the time you have left, open your mind to all possibilities. Whether you will recover or get worse or die soon is unknown, and the quality of your life will be greatly enhanced when you examine the source of these beliefs carefully. Perhaps you can prevent negative thinking from becoming a self-fulfilling prophecy.

Be flexible with your beliefs

Before Arica and Kumar left, I offered them a sage smudge to initiate our journey together, saying that though smudging was not of my heritage, we all have the right to put our own heart and meaning into a borrowed spiritual structure. Kumar mentioned that smudging was similar to the use of incense in his religion, Hinduism. The smoke from the lit end of the dried sage bundle drifted in front of us, and Arica showed Kumar how to brush the smoke onto himself with his hand. She said a blessing in Hopi for all of us, giving thanks that we would be working together.

I gave her the sage stick and suggested that she could touch the medication packet with it without lighting it, and the doctors wouldn't mind. Then, if she still wanted to light it, she could do so after the treatment, when she was home. The intention brought the healing power, I suggested, and the kachinas would understand. Flexibility is called for, not dogma.

Several years ago, I worked with a young man who was a member of a religion that believed extraterrestrials were guiding them in their lives. His psychotherapist had referred him to me for a session because I was experienced with spiritual as well as health challenges. The goal of his religion was to behave according to the principles (similar to the Ten Commandments) so one earned merits. Each merit was symbolized as a star, and worn on the shirts of the membership. This young man was sincere in his religious practice and sought ways to earn a shiny star.

He listened to the guidance of the extraterrestrials, who taught him in his sleep. The chest of his T-shirt was covered with stars. When his whole body was covered with them, he told me, the vibrations from it would signal to the extraterrestrials that he was developed enough, and they would swoop down and take him to a new dimension. As he described it, the new dimension was much like ours, except there was no poverty, illness, or war. Other than his religious beliefs, this young man was like any other college student—concerned about exams, his studies in architecture, and how to find a girlfriend. He would pass any psychological test as normal.

Just like Arica, this young man had difficulty with the school medical center when he was being evaluated for a serious illness.

He didn't want to take off his shirt with the stars for a complete exam, saying it was against his principles. I worked with him to remove his shirt and visualize the stars on his upper body during the time he was examined. His ability to be flexible in carrying out his beliefs worked for him, and the medical team could do their job.

When it is necessary, I advise people with illness to emphasize the principles and spirit of their religious beliefs, and to be adaptable with the minute details that may be causing conflict. When we are focused on healing and recovery, conflict causes stress, which is antithetical to wholeness.

About two months after I met her, Arica's symptoms of weakness and nausea increased, keeping her in bed so she couldn't come to see me, so I visited her at home. She had lost weight and was drowsy. As she sat up and brushed her hair, Kumar helped her by supporting her back.

I pulled up a chair and we meditated. Arica said she practiced the meditation I had taught her every day; she felt it took her "to a safe place" and calmed her health worries. She reported that her recent scans showed an increased number and size of liver tumors. Chemotherapy wasn't working, and excision by surgery wasn't an option. The medical team wanted to put her on the liver transplant list, but she refused. Their suggestion angered her, and she said she couldn't help becoming argumentative. "They don't respect my views," she said, "and I know they think I'm stupid and superstitious! Why can't white people accept our spiritual ways? They're prejudiced—so prejudiced." I countered that I, and many white people, value and respect the sacred paths of American Indian traditions, and that she was lumping all white people into one category, which was itself prejudicial.

"I get it. You're right. But I just can't help it when I'm

frustrated. My belief is my belief. You see, I know if you get someone's organ, you end up with their feelings and even want the food they liked. I don't want anybody's body part in me, because that person's spirit will come looking for it and be angry. I don't want to be haunted."

"Do you understand that if the tumors can't be reduced, they'll continue to grow until you die?"

"Yes, they explained all that at the hospital. I still don't want it." Arica's beliefs were keeping her from considering the life she had planned with Kumar and her career in design. She was unwilling to talk to other transplant recipients, as the doctor suggested, to test out her beliefs about being taken over by the feelings and needs of the organ donor. And her belief that white people were untrustworthy kept her from taking in information from her medical team.

At the end of the visit we did the following meditation. A friend of mine, who is a writer, has become so proficient at this exercise that he does it before creating each written piece. He says that the more he practices, the more the material flows. In addition to centering and calming your bodymind, this exercise is helpful in learning to remember dreams. It is an example of an open meditation.

Exercise: Music-Imagery Meditation

1. Find a quiet place. Have your journal and a pen nearby. Turn on some meditative music.

2. Sit or lie down in a comfortable position. Close your eyes. Relax your jaw, shoulders, and belly.

3. Take a few deep breaths and release any tension in your body.

4. As you relax even more, images will begin to enter your mind.

   Just notice the flow of images, paying attention without trying to remember or hang on to them. When thoughts enter, come back to the images. You may have a dreamlike sequence, even though you're not asleep.

5. When the music ends, pick up your journal and record what you remember. Write down images, feelings, and thoughts. Afterward, write down your associations to the images. This will take you deeper into the material and make the bridge between your conscious and unconscious minds more accessible. You will enter a flow of self-revelation and discovery that is the heart of personal transformation. You will get closer to the essence of your true self and begin to sense the wonder of the unique human being that you are.

Another meditation that has been helpful to my clients is one I practice every evening at bedtime. I find that it calms my mind and helps me let go of the day's activities. It is an open meditation, based on the space between thoughts—much like the rest stop between music notes. We place our attention on empty space rather than on an object of focus. It is free from concepts. It is restful and healing, and it connects us to the most primary state of consciousness, which is simply *being*.

Exercise: Emptiness Meditation

1. Find a quiet place. Sit in a comfortable position. Close your eyes. Relax your jaw, shoulders, and belly.

2. Take a few deep breaths and release any tension in your body.

3. Place your attention on the space between your thoughts or images. This space is pristine awareness— presence without the content of thoughts. Pure awareness will enlarge the more you practice. For me, it's like looking at a clear, pulsating, black sky. Breathe into that space and stay there as long as you can. The goal is to enlarge that spaciousness.

4. When thoughts enter, consider them as guests passing through. Release them and bring your attention again to the space between thoughts.

   This meditation may be more challenging than other types, but it is well worth the effort. With sincere practice, you may be able to achieve a minute or more of the state of consciousness that has no object or thought.

Modify your beliefs about others

Sometimes in our desire to defend our own beliefs, we misunderstand or misinterpret what others are saying and doing. This happened with Arica when I accompanied her to the hospital for a checkup. She assumed that her doctor didn't value her beliefs and never would acquiesce to her requests for incorporating her Hopi spiritual traditions into her treatments.

In the middle of the exam, her cooperative mood shifted and she became angry.

"Why don't you have native healers and medicine people in the hospital like they do in Arizona?" she complained. "You don't care about our ways or alternative health! In some hospitals they even have special rooms where patients can do ceremony or ritual dances!" Arica had slipped into a critical mode and was letting her anger rule. I put my hand on her shoulder, and she became quiet. The doctor was stunned by her outburst and looked to me for direction. "Everything is okay," I offered in a calm voice. I told her to ask for what she wanted in a different way.

"Can I have a healer work with me in the hospital?" she ventured.

"Of course," the doctor replied. "But it's important you don't take any herbs or nutrients without checking with me first, because they might interfere with our treatment. I need to know everything alternative you're doing."

As she took the courage to express her beliefs, she and her doctor agreed that there could be soft drumming in her room, but no sage or incense burning because it would drift through the halls to other patients. He told her that her name would be coming to the top of the transplant list soon. Arica was quiet. Later, I talked to her about the other people waiting for a transplant—if she refused it at the last minute, it would be too late to prepare the next recipient on the list. She was sad, saying she had never thought about those other people.

"Arica, I'm not pushing you for your decision or trying to make you feel guilty. I'm asking you to use everything you know and believe to go deeper and to find your own truth. Do your prayers, your chants, while you're here. Tonight ask for a dream to guide you. Petition your spirit helpers to give you strength. And expect that the right answer will come to you. This is something you alone can do—Kumar or I can't do it for you."

I asked Arica to petition the kachinas in her prayers, to ask if she could have the transplant and do special prayers so the donor's energies would not remain in the liver she would receive.

The next day she was excited. "It worked—what you told me to do worked. I got confirmation. In a dream I saw myself with gray hair and grown children and their children. One of the grandchildren had my name. Kumar was there, and we were all so happy. We couldn't be that happy if a ghost spirit was haunting me for its transplanted liver! I know it now. I'm sure! I can be okay with someone else's liver. I prayed and chanted and I'm going to be okay. I can have the transplant."

She had phoned her parents and told them everything, and they immediately got on a plane to be with her.

In four days Kumar called to say Arica was home, but she was very sick again and in bed. She wanted to see me. I told him to notify the doctor immediately. I canceled my other appointments and wove through traffic to the downtown area. Kumar met me at the door, panicked. "Come now," he pleaded. I walked past the roommates, who were praying and fingering their wooden bead rosaries. I passed lit candles and inhaled the scent of sandalwood from incense sticks in little pots of salt. There was a feeling of urgency everywhere.

Arica's parents were massaging her grossly swollen legs with oil. They greeted me, and the mother said she had been bathing

Arica when she went unconscious for a few minutes. Lying on the bed, she appeared very weak and her skin was a brighter yellow than I had seen before. She opened her eyes to greet me, and the whites too were a strong shade of yellow. Her breathing was shallow. She limply waved and pointed her family and Kumar to the other room, and she tugged on my skirt to have me sit on the side of her bed.

I told Kumar to call an ambulance. It was obvious she was in metabolic failure, her internal organs shutting down. I had seen it before. She told me she was in pain and was afraid. She had dreamed that the kachinas came to get her.

The next morning as I got out of the shower, the phone rang. It was Kumar. He said Arica had been given medication for her pain as soon as she was placed in her hospital room. He had stayed the night with her, and early in the morning she died. We murmured words of grief to each other, and arranged to meet.

I counseled the family and the roommates, who had become intimately involved with Arica's care. Her parents performed ritual prayers over Arica's ashes, and the next week they, Kumar, and the roommates placed her ashes into the sea. Kumar came to me for counseling several times, and I referred him to a grief group.

This young person had the courage to change her limiting beliefs and attitudes. She was able to set aside her prejudice toward white people throughout the course of our work together, in effect forgiving those who she felt had treated her poorly. She also let go of her fear of the transplant and was willing to accept treatment. She did the work to discover her rich inner resources. By accepting the support offered by her family and Kumar, she became strong and whole. I felt gratitude for the privilege of connecting intimately to these people who accompanied Arica on her journey. I knew this beautiful young woman for four months, and I will never forget her.

When you honestly address your beliefs and attitudes, you'll discover how they influence your health, well-being, and all of your life. You can ask your inner wisdom to present you with the truth, or explore your beliefs and concerns with a counselor, and you will begin to see how they may be self-limiting. And then, when you courageously take a step to open up or change the beliefs that don't serve you, you'll experience a freedom of movement that guides you along the path toward wholeness.

CHAPTER 4

Who Am I?

For what is it to die but to stand naked in the wind
and to melt into the sun?

—Kahlil Gibran, *The Prophet*

Throughout the ages, philosophers, scientists, and students of
life have addressed the question "What is a human being?"
There are many ways to answer the question, of course. One
answer is that we are organisms comprising body, mind, and
spirit. Another is that we are creatures belonging to the genus
Homo. A third answer might be that we have the characteristics
of people as opposed to plants or robots, or animals. Ultimately,
there is no one definition of a human being that would satisfy
everyone. We are very complex beings—mentally, physically,
emotionally, and spiritually.

Our perception of ourselves is equally complex. We have
ideas and feelings about who we are that are constantly changing, depending on the setting, how we're feeling and thinking,
and who we are relating to. One way of knowing ourselves is
through our subpersonalities, or selves. For example, at times I
turn into a perfectionist workhorse who is more interested in
paperwork and workshop planning than social conversation—
to the dismay of my staff. I'm conscious of goals and time

restraints and become very efficient. I've named this "office work mode" part of me Ms. Farnsworth. I feel a supercharged energy in my body and mind when she is present. Thankfully, Ms. Farnsworth never shows up when I'm counseling clients or leading a seminar or being with friends—these are not her venues. Instead, another part of me appears who is interested in everything she can learn and share with her friends and clients. This other part has open energy and is caring in relationship to others; she is not concerned with efficiency at all.

These are just a couple of my selves, or subpersonalities. I also know that I have a quiet nature girl who could live alone in the woods, surviving off the land. She has a sister, a spiritual part of me. I have a techie self who is fascinated with computers, sound systems, and everything electronic, and who would enroll me in an auto mechanics class if I let her. You already know that I enjoy living with indigenous people—my inner cultural anthropologist could let me be absorbed into a nontechnological culture for many years if I gave her free reign; she wants to learn about people at the ends of the earth, the more remote, the better. And I have an intuitive part that has access to information that doesn't come from logic; she is most active in my sessions with clients.

A multitude of selves

We all have many selves, which can easily be identified in order to get to know who we are more deeply. These selves are a natural part of our psyches. Each has a pattern of behavior, feeling, and thinking that has developed at some time in our lives to help us cope and flourish. Discovering these parts, many of which are unconscious, brings us valuable understanding about our gifts and challenges. They are key to initiating personal transformation and living a full life. (They are not to be confused with the psychiatric condition of dissociative identity disorder, or multiple personality, which is a serious psychological disorder affecting a very small percentage of the population.)

If you are facing the end of your life, you may wonder why it's important to explore the question "Who am I?" This is your time to dive into life, *your* life, and to explore yourself more deeply than ever before. In doing so, you have the opportunity for healing wounds that you may have pushed into hiding, and to find treasures and joy in yourself that you never knew existed. As you rediscover who you are from a fresh view, you may find interesting and sometimes surprising aspects of your psyche that produce an aha realization. As one of my friends said, "I'm so happy I did this work; now I can die having a clear understanding of why my life has been the way it was." Doing this deep personal work gives us the best chance for recovery from illness, if that is to happen.

So let's begin by getting a baseline view of yourself. Get out your journal and do the following exercise. Spontaneously let the words flow. Write in any way you wish—make a list or write several paragraphs or pages.

Exercise: Discover Your Primary Selves

Answer the Question: Who Am I?

After you have finished, close your eyes and invite an image of yourself that fits each description you have written.

For instance, one sentence I wrote in this exercise when I was fifteen years old was, "I am an explorer." I had an image of myself on a catamaran, sailing alone between two islands. I could feel the sun and the wind, and enjoyed the freedom of sailing and anticipated the adventure of reaching a new island. Years later, that image became reality. And now, as more time has passed and I no longer sail catamarans, my explorer self seeks other avenues. But still I can bring alive this particular experience of being an explorer at sea by activating that energy in myself and call forth the image of sailing a catamaran between two islands. It's a vital part of who I am, and I want to keep it alive.

Review what you have written in the previous exercise. How interesting that you have chosen these descriptions of yourself. Perhaps you were surprised at what you've included or left out. Work with your material a bit—is there anything else you'd like to add? Title your writing "Primary Selves."

Voice Dialogue and the psychology of selves

One of my favorite methods to use with my clients is Voice Dialogue, a system developed by Drs. Sidra and Hal Stone to explore the subpersonalities each of us has in our psyche. In this method, a facilitator helps the client become aware of and experience the many selves that may be unconscious but that have the power to run our lives. By becoming conscious of these selves, we can learn to use them to make changes in our lives. It is a unique and elegant technique, different from other therapies utilizing the concept of selves.

During a Voice Dialogue session, which you'll learn about later in this chapter, we invite individual parts, or selves, to come forward to speak about what was relevant for them at this time. When I facilitate clients in this technique, each time they move from part to part they physically move to a separate chair or place on the couch. Each self carries a distinct energy and feeling, and I ask my clients to experience that energy to the best of their abilities.

Primary selves

In growing up each of us develops characteristic ways of thinking and feeling and acting that become familiar to us. In Voice Dialogue we call these our "primary selves," and these primary selves define us; they are who we are in the world. These selves protect us—and our deepest feelings and sensitivities—and enable us to function. From your writing in the previous exercise you should have a good feeling for yours. I had a client whose primary selves were all about maintaining power—power at work, power over his family. Everywhere and with everyone, he needed to be in charge. Through Voice Dialogue he discovered a vulnerable self who didn't enjoy power at all, who wanted to be taken care of. At first he was embarrassed when this part came forward in our work, but soon he learned to show his gentle side to his wife and children, which made everyone happier. From his Aware Ego, he could recognize the feelings and energies of his gentle self, and could choose when it was safe to express it.

Disowned selves

On the other hand, for every self that we identify with, there are one or more selves that have been rejected or disowned. We don't consciously know about these disowned selves or how they might possibly be operating in us. Or if we are conscious of them stirring within us, we feel uncomfortable and reject them as quickly and definitively as possible.

These disowned selves carry what we are missing in our lives, and they are often just what we need for a sense of completion as our lives draw to an end. They can bring us the gifts that we (or our primary selves) didn't even know we needed. But how do we discover our disowned selves? The following exercise will help you uncover them.

Again, let yourself write without hesitation or thinking too much—just keep writing. Everything is important, so include all details. I use the example of a domineering brother, but you will find your own examples from your own life.

Exercise: Identifying Your Disowned Selves

1. Imagine someone you tend to judge—someone who pushes your buttons, who really irritates you. Picture this person and sit with your emotions and sensations, both mental and physical, when you think of this person. Write down what comes to mind.

2. Try to isolate the precise quality this person has that you dislike the most. What, exactly, is so dreadful

about this person? Your reaction will probably be visceral. The more disowned this self is, the stronger our emotional reaction, and the more we feel this reaction in the body itself. Write down all the details.

3. The quality of feeling or behavior you judge in another is in fact a picture of what is disowned in your own life. If you discover you can't stand your older brother because he is "dominating" and a "know-it-all," and you constantly live in judgment of him, then you learn that he carries your disowned self. Each of us contains the full spectrum of selves, and the disowned ones reside in our unconscious. You may never express your dominating or know-it-all self, but there she is, vibrating in your unconscious, sometimes reacting when she sees herself mirrored by another person. That reaction comes out as judgment of the other's overt behavior. Through writing, explore how these qualities show up in you.

4. Now you are free to take the next step. Your disowned self is the part of you that, like your brother, knows all the answers and enjoys being in charge. What you judge and feel hatred for in the world lives inside you, operating underground. Describe in writing specific examples of when you've wanted to be in charge and weren't able to claim your power to do so.

5. As you begin to see that your brother carries your disowned self, you can start to witness your primary self. If you have disowned the qualities of domination and being a know-it-all, perhaps you have grown up valuing the qualities of being nice, fair, and loving: You don't want to show off; you don't want to push others

around or hurt their feelings; you don't want to make them feel bad about themselves. But when you are in the presence of someone like your brother, you find yourself unable to make yourself heard. You can't honor your own needs or your own knowledge. Write down one of your primary selves and your disowned self that is its opposite.

6. Now picture and write about what it would be like to have just a little bit of your "powerful" brother in your life. How might your life be different? How might you react differently to others? What difficult situations might be resolved? What would it be like to have people pay attention to you? Where in your life might you take charge? *Integrating our disowned selves does not mean becoming them or behaving like the person we can't stand.* It simply means knowing we have these selves and need to learn how to use them in a new and conscious way. You need not become your brother; merely claim a little of the positive side of his way of being in the world. We can achieve this by intending to be aware of these energies, and dialoguing with them without judgment. They are usually eager to come forward and be known. The exercises in this chapter will help you get to know them.

7. Write down other parts of yourself that you feel are disowned or undeveloped. They may be your artist, or adventurer, or scholar. You may have disowned the part of you that likes to strictly keep rules, or maybe you don't have a developed inner critic. Label this exercise "Disowned Parts."

If you do nothing more than identify and explore your primary and disowned selves, you will have mapped out a significant part of who you are. This is a fundamental practice in Voice Dialogue. The work is ongoing and always exciting. You'll find that you intuitively choose the appropriate descriptor to fit the part of you that functions in a particular way.

The Aware Ego

The goal is to get to know each part fully and to develop what is called the Aware Ego, a dynamic part of consciousness that functions as a witness to all the selves and understands and holds the tensions and oppositions among them. The Aware Ego is separate from and values each self, and is neither judgmental nor preferential. It clearly can see the dynamics of each part and how the parts interact. The understanding that comes from a developed Aware Ego can help free us from being trapped under the influence of one particular part. From the position of the Aware Ego, we see the truth of what's happening with our selves, and can make adjustments.

Universal selves

Remember, each self is an energy dynamic that operates in our psyches. Its expression may have unique qualities, but the energy pattern operates similarly in all people. In Jungian psychology these energy patterns are called "archetypes." Here are a few main selves that we all have:

Mother or father—the nurturing aspect within all people. Their negative expressions show up as the *matriarch* and *patriarch*, who are dictatorial and distant.

Vulnerable child—the part that is innocent, open to the world, and undefended. This self knows about love. He wants to relate to others openly and needs to be protected. The child also shows up in other forms, such as the *rebellious child*. The *creative child* is highly active in every person, young or adult, and lets his creative juices flow.

Pusher—the industrious one who gets things done, advances at work, and excels at school. Everyone who gets through college or has a successful career has an inner pusher with big muscles. Sometimes this part pushes to the point of exhaustion, upsetting balance in one's life.

Wise woman or man—the part that has access to wisdom states. She has an overview of life. She is the voice of experience within that knows what to say and do, and makes good choices. In the extreme, this voice can be overly authoritative and intimidating.

Inner critic—the voice within us that tells us what we have done wrong, where we have missed the mark, and that we'll never be good enough. The critic can be very destructive and pervasive. This usually is an internalized voice of one or both parents or an authority figure in our childhood. The inner critic sometimes operates from our unconscious— we are not aware that we habitually criticize ourselves and fail to recognize our own beauty, intelligence, or creativity.

Another form of the critic is the judgment voice, the one that puts down others. Through Voice Dialogue work, the inner critic can fade from its position as a primary self, but we can retain its useful ability to notice differences—discernment.

Spiritual self—This part is in contact with universal transpersonal energies and the sacred. Its purpose is devotion to a higher power and service to others. When this is a primary self, sometimes the personal self suffers.

Saboteur—The saboteur can block our growth and success, usually with subtle, unconscious maneuvers. A positive quality of this voice that you may want to keep as it loses its power is the ability to create boundaries.

Lover—This part seeks unity. Its primary purpose is to engage with others and with every activity, and to create harmony among people and within oneself. When this part runs the show, sometimes keeping boundaries is a problem.

Perfectionist—The perfectionist seeks excellence, pays attention to details, and is not happy until things are arranged in the best possible way. You can see how these qualities are helpful in all endeavors. But in the extreme, this energy hampers movement and choice, or becomes obsessive. The perfectionist often operates in concert with the pusher.

Victim—The victim feels that life has dealt him a raw deal. He constantly complains about being treated unfairly. When this energy is a primary self, anything that doesn't work out for this person is blamed on others.

⌒

There are many other parts that carry specific energy and behavioral patterns: tyrannical selves, those who block movement toward wholeness, caretaker selves, etc. It doesn't matter what you name them; the important thing is to learn to notice when they are taking over and not allowing other parts to come through. For example, being in the energy of nurturing mother is appropriate and beautiful when interacting with your children, but if this is the only way you relate to your mate, the relationship will soon be in trouble—no husband or wife wants to be treated like a child.

In people with terminal or increasingly debilitating illness, the victim self is either active as a primary self or is disowned and unconscious. I have worked with several clients who were quite vociferous about how unfair it was that they were ill. Their inner victims were strong primary selves. One man, Brad, even argued that it should have been his twin brother who got liver disease, since Brad was the one who had done more good in life, while his brother had "wasted his life with nonsense." Brad suffered greatly in his predominant view of himself as a victim, feeling everything and everyone in the world conspired to keep him down. Everyone with illness has a story about why they got ill, and Brad was stuck in his story of being a victim.

When we worked with Voice Dialogue, Brad was appalled at how much his victim self influenced his relationships and ran his life. He was able to bring other parts forward and became much happier with the new sense of balance in his psyche. Others responded to the change, and were more open and loving with him. His relationship with his brother deepened, so both felt they were back to their childhood closeness.

Some of my ill clients have disowned their victim self so much that they are unable to feel anger or sadness about their deteriorating lives. They develop primary selves with a "stiff upper lip" and never complain about pain or show distress. They may be seen as model patients by their health care team. They believe they are being kind and making it easier on the people they love, but they are not being kind to themselves. Denial traps energy in the bodymind that needs to be flowing. I encourage them to express feelings of unfairness and anger about their illness with a trusted person, so they can come into balance.

Remember, each self contains a gift and a challenge. Our individual selves are not good or bad, and we don't want to kill off any one of them. Rather, we want to bring them into balance. Ideally we live and express through our many selves. This balance is achieved through developing an Aware Ego in Voice Dialogue.

Voice Dialogue dreamwork

There are many ways to begin working with Voice Dialogue, and one way is through dreamwork. When you are plunged into the confusing emotional morass of terminal or increasingly debilitating illness, working with Voice Dialogue dreamwork can offer hope—perhaps not for physical healing, but hope that you can identify and learn to manage the contradictory dynamics your psyche exhibits under duress.

I used dreamwork with Voice Dialogue to help a client of mine named Gerald.

Gerald was fifty years old and had lived alone for the past fifteen years after his wife divorced him. He told me she had left because she felt he was a child, incapable of relating to her as an adult husband.

A formerly active surfer, Gerald had serious health issues. His arteries were almost completely occluded with plaque and his heart was too weak for surgery. His cardiologist had told him he wouldn't survive the next cardiac event that would certainly occur, and that he should prepare for death and enjoy his life in the months he had left. Gerald said he didn't think about dying, even though he was short of breath and weak if he moved around too much. He rarely left his garage apartment. He had been a high school math teacher, and still did a little tutoring in his home. When I asked him to describe his view of life, he described it as "shitty."

I explained to him the value of dreamwork in revealing unconscious processes that influence and often direct our behavior. He was interested in the idea that the unconscious affects our health, relationships, and journey in life.

Gerald said he had never been in therapy or done inner work, but that he was intrigued by dreams. He told me his most recent dream:

> I was driving along in an old car, a classic MG that
> was a bright green convertible. The top was down and
> I was speeding down a winding mountain road. All of
> a sudden it started to rain so much that I couldn't see
> in front of me. I was shivering and tried to see a place

where I could pull off the road, but I knew the edge of the road was a cliff that dropped far down into a crevasse. There was no place to stop, so I kept going. Then the rain turned to hail. It hurt when it hit me on the head, and without thinking, I put my arms up over my head. I was entering a sharp curve, so I grabbed the wheel and slammed on the brakes. I skidded into a truck that was stopped around the curve. Right into the back of it.

The driver, a really big guy, came around the back of the truck toward me. He was carrying a tire iron in one hand and a flashlight in the other, and he looked really mad. I didn't know what to do. I started apologizing when he got close to my car. He looked at me and asked if I was hurt and if he could help me. I was surprised. He wasn't mad at all. He and I pushed my car backward, because it was jammed under the truck, in between the back tires. It was hard in the rain and bursts of hail. Then he called a tow truck on his radio—my cell phone didn't work on the mountain. He let me wait in his truck until the tow came. It ended there.

Placing him in the middle of the couch, I told him that in this spot he was the Gerald that everyone knew, the person who contained multiple selves, or parts.

"Okay, close your eyes and remember the scene where you are in your car when it was stuck under the back wheels of the reefer. See the driver coming toward you in the rain and notice everything about him—the way he walks, his facial expression, the flashlight and tire iron in his hands."

"Got it."

I invited him to move to his left or right on the couch, to occupy the space where the truck driver self would sit. He moved a few inches to the left.

"Now imagine you are the driver, in his body, sitting here. Feel his physical structure. He is a part of you, since you dreamed of him. Take your time, and if you feel him or his energy, open your eyes and I'll talk with you, the truck driver who's a part of Gerald."

"Hi," he said after a moment. His voice was lower and stronger than Gerald's.

"I understand you helped Gerald when he ran into your truck in the dream."

"Yeah, I did," the driver replied.

"Tell me about yourself. The dream Gerald was surprised you weren't angry."

"Yeah. Everybody thinks I'm tough, but I'm not. I'm a big guy and look tough and talk rough, but really all I want to do is help people. I go to church and we learn about loving others, even when they do bad things."

"Do you have a temper?"

"No, I don't. But some other part of Gerald does."

"How does temper show up in Gerald's life?"

"It doesn't. I can't let him go around hurting people, so I hold it in."

"That must be hard."

We continued our conversation. The truck driver recounted several instances in Gerald's childhood in which he was hurt or disappointed by his family and others. In these instances, the truck driver self stepped in and presented a persona of tough indifference, while holding back anger. When the energy of the driver waned, I asked him to move back into the seat of Gerald. We were silent for a moment.

"How was that?" I asked.

"Man . . . that's different. I liked it. It feels right on—a tough part of me that's holding in anger. I'm so surprised—it's real."

"And related to that toughness is a desire to be in a loving world."

I asked Gerald to move to a new place on the couch. I suggested he go inward to sense the young part of himself who had been hurt. "In this work," I said, "if you don't feel the energy coming forward, then we'll move to another part. Nothing should be forced. And sometimes when we're looking for one energy, another self appears. So we go with that one."

He became the vulnerable child. His voice softened and his body drew inward. He said he was five years old. This was a risk for Gerald, and I was proud of his willingness to go into this dialogue. What emerged was a picture of a tender, sensitive child who was ignored by his parents. As a child, he looked to his surfing coach for affection and encouragement, and tried to get attention at school by misbehaving. He had few friends because it was difficult for him to trust. Being on the ocean was his major source of happiness, he told me.

"Does Gerald let you come out much now?" I asked.

"No. Not now."

"I suppose that truck driver keeps you quiet."

He sighed and looked into my eyes. "All the time."

"What do you want Gerald to know about you?"

He was silent, then said, "I want him to remember me. To be loving and feel me, just like when he's riding a big wave. He should know what I need. I want to be happy, to play more. With people—with a girlfriend. I want him to get a girlfriend. That'd be nice. And I want him to stop fighting with his son, Jim. Don't like the fights. It's scary. And more ice cream—chocolate. And no more cigarettes, 'cause they're nasty and make you sick."

I alternated speaking with the driver, the child, and Gerald. As the driver, he broke down after ranting about the anger he had toward Gerald's parents. I moved him into child, where he cried and said how alone and afraid he felt, knowing no one was protecting him. This was a key dynamic, so I proceeded slowly, allowing the child periods of silence as he shared. I stayed closely connected to him so he would feel supported.

"Thank you for talking with me," I said. "I'm sure your message was heard. Now, please move back into Gerald."

He moved back to the center seat, his original position, clasped his hands between his knees, and bent his head down. "Thanks," he said, "that was amazing. I felt so young." From this position of his Aware Ego, we discussed Gerald's experience, noting how the driver and child were related. The Aware Ego was the one who was centered and could integrate the work we had just done with the other selves.

One of the things Voice Dialogue allows us to do is to check in regularly with the parts of our personalities we discover through the process. The goal is not to change the parts, but to experience their thoughts, feelings, and energies. By attending to the selves individually in this way, the Aware Ego process begins to develop and one has the choice of which self to bring forward at any given time. Then the selves no longer rule our lives unconsciously.

Voice Dialogue is ideal when we feel disconnected from our experiences and feelings, as was the case with Gerald. And when we are faced with something as difficult as our own mortality, even the most self-aware and advanced practitioners of spiritual and psychological growth have the urge to shut down, to turn away. Voice Dialogue is a very special means of reconnecting with our self—actually, our many selves. Rather than trying to change the parts of ourselves that are hard on us or unpleasant, we find a centered place (the Aware Ego) from which to observe the relationships between aspects of ourselves. I have found that these selves or voices are particularly inclined to reveal themselves and to speak in the deeply transformative time of terminal illness. When we attend to these selves in session with a facilitator or transcribe what they say in a solo Voice Dialogue exchange, we are freed from any unconscious parts that are running our process.

Exploring your daydreams

Daydreams are another route to discovering which selves are disowned or undeveloped. One way to do this exercise is to ask yourself: What is it that I find irresistibly attractive in a particular person? What does he or she have that I don't have in my life? Or, what are my daydreams?

Everyone spends time daydreaming. As you walk down the street, you might find yourself imagining a conversation with someone at work. In the fantasy, you are angry and aggressive with them. You act the opposite of the way you actually would when interacting with the person. In everyday life, you would never, ever behave in this way, because you are a reasonable and cooperative person. This is a common fantasy for someone who feels disempowered at work. Our fantasies are valuable teachers, pointing us toward areas of learning. And they appear automatically, a gift from the unconscious.

So find a quiet place and time where you can check into your own fantasies to see what you can learn from them. The following steps are another way, through daydreams, to help you discover your disowned or undeveloped selves. This concept of disowned selves needs repetition and practice; it's at the core of all Voice Dialogue work.

Exercise: Your Daydream Self

1. Close your eyes and move into the space of a daydream you have had often. Feel what it is like to be this particular version of self. The "you" in the daydream also gives you a picture of your disowned selves. Perhaps in real life you are always very nice when talking to people at work. In the daydream, it is the opposite—the disowned self in action.

2. Come closer to this daydream self—the aggressive "you" who tells people what he or she thinks—and imagine what it might be like if you incorporated some of that self into your work. Place yourself in the scene and feel yourself embodied there. How might things be different if you were more assertive at work? How might you react differently to others? What might you say, what might you suggest, what might you do?

Write down your feelings, thoughts, and images in your journal. Perhaps you want to give this part a name.

3. Repeat this exercise by getting in touch with another fantasy you've had about yourself. Whether it is singing beautifully to an appreciative audience or rock-climbing to the peak of Mont Blanc, enter the daydream fully. Feel the energies of this part of yourself that has not been expressed, and enjoy it. There is no judgment, no matter what the fantasy is. You are incorporating your disowned or undeveloped selves.

Your selves in relationship

In Gerald's Voice Dialogue session, his vulnerable inner child didn't like Gerald's fighting with Jim, his son. There always was an uncomfortable tension between the two men, which was even more awkward because Gerald was dependent on Jim for shopping and transportation to medical appointments. Jim held resentment toward Gerald for not being present in his life when he needed him to be a father, and now the positions were reversed. They fought regularly and loudly when Jim criticized his father's excessive drinking and smoking and general lack of self-care. The fact that Gerald wasn't expected to live long exacerbated the unhappy feelings between father and son, because everything was unresolved. However, when I worked with them, I could see that underneath all the discord, they cared for each other and both were fearful of the probability that Gerald would die soon.

In our sessions it became apparent that in their relationship, Jim was acting out of his *inner critical father.* He made clear his disapproval of Gerald's living style and his drinking and smoking. There was a tone of disdain when he spoke, as if he were telling his dad, "This is what I have to endure with you! You should do what I tell you." Gerald was equally defensive, acting out of his *inner rebellious son.* He ignored Jim's suggestions and gave flippant answers. Neither was connecting to the other.

Bonding patterns

Their critical father/rebellious son relationship is what we call a "bonding pattern." A bonding pattern is an interaction of power selves and disempowered selves between two people or more. In this case, Jim was exhibiting the power in the relationship through his strong criticism. Gerald then felt disempowered, so he retreated into his rebellious child and reacted defensively in a childish way. They got caught in this pattern every time they met. It left no room for vulnerability in Gerald and Jim's relationship, the place where two people meet as partners in a fluid and healthy relationship. Although every relationship always involves the parent/child dynamic, Jim had taken his chosen role of parent to a dictatorial extreme, and in turn, his father took on the role of child in a rebellious way.

Exercise: Examine Your Relationships

Our relationships play a big part in shaping who we are. Understanding how they work gives us insight into ourselves.

In your journal, write the names of three people whom you feel closest to. For each one, write about:

1. What is the balance of power in this relationship? Who feels the need to be in charge most of the time? How does this happen? What happens if the other pushes to regain power? What are your feelings about this?

2. What are you giving up in this relationship that you'd like to reclaim?

3. How vulnerable and open are you willing to be with each person? How does this show up? Is the other person vulnerable with you? Would you like to change your level of vulnerability and intimacy?

4. How has your illness affected these relationships? Are you in a negative bonding pattern with someone in your family or a caretaker?

Read what you have written. When we examine our relationships we can see that they are very complex. We know from our day-to-day living what works and what doesn't in each one. And now that we can begin to think in terms of primary and disowned selves, it's easier to understand some of the deeper dynamics. The most important thing to remember is to embrace each part of yourself; with this acceptance comes understanding and compassion for how each has developed. This understanding can lead to transformation of our relationships, so they become healthier and more alive. Some of the most dramatic, positive changes I've seen have come when both parties in a relationship work with the principles of Voice Dialogue.

Get to know your inner child

The young parts of ourselves play a major role when we are dealing with illness, especially illness that is life threatening. Because they are the essence of our vulnerability, they feel unsafe and afraid with the prospects of treatment, disability, disempowerment, and death. Our inner children come in many forms, from the creative child to the shy child to the gregarious child, and so on. They all fear isolation and abandonment and react instinctively to protect themselves. When they are disturbed, they may act out and become rebellious, unruly, and hyperemotional. They are children being children. It can be confusing when you find yourself behaving like this, and equally confusing to those who have never experienced your inner child if you have kept this part of yourself hidden. To our power selves—the ones who have to be in control—the child may seem like a weak or distasteful part that needs to be shut down. But the best way to treat our vulnerable child is to let it speak and express. Once the child's fears and concerns are addressed, it feels safer and has less of a need to shout loudly. Of course, our child also can come out in loving, sensitive ways without any disturbing behavior.

When Gerald and I worked with his inner child, we discovered gold. I had left him pastels to draw with, and at my next visit, he showed me his artwork. They were primitive renderings of the ocean waves, beach scenes, several futuristic versions of surfboards, and at the bottom of the pile, a drawing of stick figures. "Tell me about that," I asked. It was a typical child's drawing of his family. He said the two tall figures, which filled the height of the page, were his parents. Pointing to a tiny figure in the corner, he said, "That's me. I'm hiding."

When I inquired why he was hiding, he said he was always hiding from his parents so they couldn't make him go to parochial school. He hated the uniforms, the strict nuns, the sanctions against comic books, and the daily chapel attendance. "Those nuns were mean. They didn't let me talk about things I liked, and thought we should pray all the time instead of having fun. They tried to ruin my spirit. Between them and my parents, I had no freedom, no choice. I was nothing. I wasn't the kid my parents wanted—a studious, religious, good boy. I wanted to be outside and free. When I cooperated at home and school I was a puppet. No one ever gave me a break."

I suggested he probably developed sarcasm to get back at authoritative parents and teachers, to protect himself, and to feel empowered in a somewhat safe way. He agreed, saying when the nuns had punished him, he nearly always got in more trouble for his subsequent whispered retorts. In high school, some classmates admired his sarcastic wit. "A few friends were the only ones who weren't against me," he said. "The rest of the world was." I told him I could understand why he had difficulty relating to his son, given his own background. I explained that even though the specifics were different, his pattern of ignoring his son's needs was the same as his parents not caring for his. Without awareness, the pattern gets passed on to succeeding generations. By doing the following exercise, you will learn more about your inner child and the influence he or she has on your life.

Exercise: Connect to Your Inner Child

Choose a time when you can do this work without being disturbed. It should be in a place where you feel safe and comfortable. Have your journal, a pad of art paper, and some oil pastels or crayons with you. You also might want to play some gentle music in the background.

1. Start with some deep breathing—seven belly breaths. Relax your jaw, shoulders, and belly, letting go of any tension in your body.

2. Close your eyes. Recall a time when you were young. Feel yourself in that body, noticing what you are wearing and where you are. Look around and notice all the details in your mind. Perhaps there are other people present. Let yourself explore and interact in this scene. What or whom are you attracted to? Notice how you feel.

3. Open your eyes and draw this young self. Draw the surrounding environment. Draw confidently and easily in your own way.

4. In your journal, write a story about your drawing. It may be a true version of what you remember, or something you make up now. Don't worry about the accuracy. Write about all the details.

5. Write about what you as the child in the drawing felt. What did this part of you need then? What does this part need and want now?

6. Imagine that you are holding your inner child. Talk to him or her—have a conversation by writing in your journal. Alternate between your voice and the child's, writing down the statements and responses. End by giving reassurance that you will be here for him or her—that you'll stay connected.

7. Write anything else about this that comes to mind.

8. Read, review, and process what you've learned about
    your inner child.

How to use self-awareness to deepen relationships

You now have a basic understanding of two key dynamics in every relationship: the power dynamic and the need for and protection of vulnerability, which is necessary for intimacy. They are at opposite ends of the continuum and constantly shift in any given relationship. You have identified and worked with various parts of yourself. You know about your primary and disowned selves. And you understand the importance of developing an Aware Ego, which is able to see the interactions among all your selves. Now you are well equipped to begin to heal those relationships that are unsatisfactory or imbalanced. This is especially important because we want to be able to enjoy quality time with those around us when death is imminent.

Go back to the exercise called Examine Your Relationships. Think of the first person you wrote about. The healing starts with self-honesty. Where is the power and who carries the vulnerability? Are both of you battling for power and blocking vulnerability? Recognize if you have gotten caught in a bonding pattern. Can you find a way to accept your part as one side of the equation in the dysfunctional relationship? Hopefully, you also have identified a relationship you have that is not caught in a bonding pattern, in which the power is shared and both parties are able to connect through vulnerability.

Begin to think in terms of the selves interacting in your

relationship, and start with yourself. For instance, a friend of mine told me that her strong "inner bitch" was coming out too often with her mate. She also was aware of her strong pleaser, who came forward and worked overtime to please her partner after her bitch subpersonality wreaked havoc. She wanted to learn to avoid swinging between the two extremes. Through our Voice Dialogue work, she learned to recognize the beginning stirrings of her inner bitch, which cued her to shift into the position of an Aware Ego. From here, she was then able to realize the dynamics of what was happening between her and her partner, and was able to make better choices in terms of how to communicate and interact with him.

Here's a personal example. When I began teaching workshops, I was upset that my sister, Judy, and I were getting into more and more arguments about things that really weren't important. We were in a negative bonding pattern. When I replayed the most recent argument in my mind, I saw that at the beginning of the conversation I was exhibiting all the power. My voice and tone were authoritative, and I wasn't connecting to her—I was speaking at her. This made her angry, and the argument started. I was holding all the power, and she felt vulnerable and small. When we discussed it, she told me that I was using my "teaching voice," as if I were lecturing in an auditorium, and she didn't want to feel like my student; she wanted to feel like my sister. She was right. I had fallen into a bad habit, and when we were arguing I was in my "teacher" part, which I should have left back at the seminar. I was unconscious of this behavior. So I elicited her help in training myself out of this bad habit and becoming more conscious of my connection to her and others. I asked her to raise her index finger slightly anytime she heard that teacher tone in my voice. I would notice and make the shift—it would be so subtle that if others were around, only we would know what was being communicated. It worked beautifully. After a few weeks of practicing with Judy, I was able to consciously and easily move into a more intimate connection with her and my friends without my teacher self interfering.

After you have identified the positive or negative bonding patterns in your relationships, you can work on clarifying your communication. Begin to speak your truth to people in terms of what you feel, want, and need, without blaming the other. Say, "I want to change the way we've been interacting. I've been looking at my part of the problem, and wonder if you're interested in improving our friendship." Continue with specifics. For example, "I don't like it when you remind me about my doctor appointments. Trust me to manage my treatment schedule, and I'll ask for help when I need it. I know you're trying to be helpful, but I can do this."

Honest communication does wonders and has a healing effect. Illness and death are challenging enough without the burden of unspoken feelings. Of course, the honest statements should be delivered with kindness and nonjudgment.

With work, Gerald and Jim healed their differences. Gerald understood that his rebellious inner child was reacting against Jim's inner patriarch. Jim learned to soften the way he talked to his father, and Gerald learned not to rebel instinctively with the sarcasm that came from his inner child. Finally they were able to enjoy each other's company, and they achieved an intimate relationship.

It's difficult enough to care for someone who is dying, but it's particularly challenging for children to care for their parents at the end of their lives. All the lifelong issues between parent and child become magnified, and sometimes parents have a hard time with the reversal of power that occurs in these situations. Being able to frankly discuss emotional hurdles helps clear the air and clarify each person's role in resolving the many issues involved when someone is dying. Every family member or caretaker should be as honest and transparent as possible, because the dying person is hypersensitive and knows what's true. He or she wants the truth, not to be coddled.

Gerald and Jim healed their relationship by going through the difficult process of finally speaking their truths. They then stopped their cautious dance with each other, and genuine behavioral changes occurred naturally. After several sessions, their vulnerability opened and they could meet each other in a place of genuine love. They expressed their trust and love of each other, and when Jim said he forgave his father, it was the first time I saw them embrace.

A few weeks later I sensed the end was near, so again I brought up the subject of death. Gerald said he was afraid, that he didn't want to suffer. "Damned if I'm going out like a blubbering baby," he said. "That would be uncool." He continued, "It doesn't seem real to me. Dead? What does that really mean?"

I said that crying about leaving his life was normal, and I assured him that beneath the fear, every person knows how to die—it's as natural as being born. I told him the Welsh myth of Dylan Eil Ton, a sea god:

> A woman gave birth to twins. She arranged a naming
> ceremony at the seashore with a high priest, to give
> thanks for her healthy boys. As the priest began his

incantations, one twin, Dylan, jumped out of his mother's arms and dove into the sea. He immediately began swimming, showing that the sea was his true home. Some say he was a shape-shifter and became a large fish, while others say he kept his human form until manhood. He was a powerful swimmer, and folks would stand on shore to see him plowing through the waves, surfing a crest, or playfully flipping into the air.

"Perhaps death is like this," I suggested. "We leave one form and become another. Dylan easily dove into the sea and embraced his new home." Gerald said he wasn't interested in talking about an afterlife, because he didn't think there was one. But he found comfort in the idea that it was an organic process and he wouldn't have to figure out how to do it. He wanted his bed moved into the living room so he could see people walking to the beach through his front window; he didn't want any music, ceremony, or anything read to him in his final days. "Just quiet," he said. "Nothing special. I want Jim and you to be there."

He took my hand and thanked me for the work we had done together.

"I feel satisfied and happy," he said, "like I've eaten a whole pizza that tasted great. And what I have with Jim now . . ." His eyes misted over. "It's the best thing that's ever happened to me."

Gerald felt whole and complete, ready to surrender his life. I was there the afternoon he died. Going in and out of consciousness, he spoke words and sentences I couldn't understand. When Jim left for a while I moved my chair closer to the bed. I placed my hand lightly on his and centered in my heart, sending him the energy of unconditional love. And just before his heart stopped, I heard him clearly say, "I'm swimming."

In this chapter you've learned a lot about your many selves—who they are, how they interact, and how they influence your life. This is a lifelong exploration. And when you learn to value each of your selves and can dialogue with them to bring them into balance, you will have taken a major stride toward achieving wholeness.

CHAPTER 5

The Heart Center

The moment you have in your heart this extraordinary thing called love and feel the depth, the delight, the ecstasy of it, you will discover that for you the world is transformed.

—Jiddu Krishnamurti

From the beginnings of Far Eastern religions to modern thought movements, the qualities and practices of love have been categorized, debated, and incorporated into cultural norms. The early Chinese philosophy of Taoism, for example, emphasizes love, or compassion, as one of the Three Jewels of the Tao—moderation and humility being the others.

Another important text about love is Plato's philosophical *Symposium*, written around 380 BCE. It is about men participating in a gathering—a drinking party—where each has to deliver a speech praising love. Phaedrus speaks of Eros (erotic love), and about the self-sacrificing love of entering battle, which honors the gods. Socrates talks about how to become a philosopher, or lover of wisdom, and some scholars also attribute the origin of the concept of Platonic love (affectionate love for a friend) to his speech. One after another, the speakers present their views and challenge the others about the meaning of filial and parental love, homosexual and heterosexual romantic love, agape or love of all humanity (unconditional love) and divine love. All argue about which is the "highest" form of love. They discuss how jealousy and anger are related to love gone wrong.

Agathon gives a poetic speech—which Socrates gently mocks—saying that love is discerning and only seeks a garden to visit where there is a bud to bloom. He also declares, "Love is simply the name for the desire and pursuit of the whole." *Symposium* is one of the first significant secular texts about love. Also, it addresses the many types of love, rather than emphasizing divine love, which was the main focus of early religious writings.

Love is a basic human need, a tremendous challenge for most people, and probably the most popular theme of books, TV shows, movies, music, and other media. Religions, psychology, and the self-help industry expound it. Technology has entered the field too—not only do we have online dating; we even have apps for our mobile devices to reveal the proximity of someone who is available for a sexual encounter.

But it is agape, or unconditional love, that leads us to transformation, that total renovation of consciousness. The Persian poet Rumi beautifully expressed the essential nature of love more than one thousand years ago when he not only wrote ecstatic verses about the longings of one human being for another and our love for the divine but also expressed the beauty of selfless love for all humanity.

There are many well-known teachers and writers who have dedicated their lives to the subject of the heart center. A modern teacher of unconditional love, William Brugh Joy, M.D., was my friend and colleague. He was a master at inducting his students into this selfless love with no preferences and no conditions.

In the last year of his life, Brugh took a pilgrimage to Mount Kailash, in Tibet. While he was there, his guide brought him to visit an ancient wise woman in one of the nearby villages. When they entered her hut, she took one look at Brugh, smiled, and said, "Ahhh. Heart priest."

In those two words she spoke to the essence of Brugh and his life's work. In his midthirties, he left his profession as a successful medical doctor to embark on his lifelong path as a teacher and spiritual guide. In the ensuing thirty-five years, he became a beloved explorer of the mystical realms of existence and the labyrinth of the human psyche. For him, the absolute bedrock of all his work was what he called the "heart center."

Brugh taught that there were four foundational aspects of the heart center—healing presence, innate harmony, supernal (divine) compassion, and unconditional love. As a "heart priest," Brugh would guide individuals into an encounter with unconditional love along with the other aspects of the heart center. For him, unconditional love was far more fundamental than the interpersonal way most of us tend to think of it (i.e. loving another no matter what). Instead, he tended to speak of it more from the perspective of a kind of mystical physicist. He believed unconditional love is the mysterious, conscious primary force that is energy transforming into matter, and matter transforming into energy.

Now, all that may seem very intellectual, but at this point there are really only two implications to appreciate about Brugh's teaching about unconditional love. First, that the fabric of all the realms of existence is composed of love. Second, each of us has the potential to experience it directly.

Whenever Brugh himself came into contact with unconditional love, he attained access to wisdom, heightened perception, healing, and many other resources, but by far his overwhelming response to it was to become filled to overflowing with a sensation that he could only describe as "wonderment." In fact, he often referred to unconditional love as "that which enables us to fall in love with the mystery itself." And from here, he was able to greet both the light and the dark, the beatific and the gruesome, the living and the dead, with presence and uncommon grace. Brugh's teachings of unconditional love live on in the hearts and practices of thousands of his students worldwide, many of whom are teachers and writers of the heart space themselves.

In my own work I have found that people hunger for unconditional love. It is a state of being that is available to us always; all we have to do is shift our awareness into this energy that is always present. To be able to tap into the feeling, knowing, and *experience* of unconditional love is the most powerful gift you can give yourself. Your whole world is transformed once you can shift your awareness into this energy of balance, wholeness, and peace. In relationships, this pure love is given without expectation of getting anything back. There are no limits or conditions on the giving, and to receive it is bliss. Perhaps the hardest of all is to love ourselves unconditionally. This means we have positive regard and appreciation for all of who we are, no matter our challenges or the mistakes we believe we have made. When you enter the state of unconditional love, you rise above the level of your problems and into a state of wholeness.

A young friend of mine, Mitsuko, changed her life when I taught her about unconditional love. When I responded to her ad offering classical guitar lessons, we got along right away. She was a good teacher and I loved playing duets with her, so our friendship deepened quickly. Because I saw her often, it soon became apparent that she was struggling with a psychiatric disorder that exhibited panic attacks as one of its symptoms. She was being treated with medication, but often skipped her dose because she said it interfered with the accuracy of her guitar playing. Many times our lesson was interrupted when she suddenly ran to the corner of the room and crouched there in abject fear. Each time it took longer to help quiet her crying and guide her into deep breathing. Her illness was becoming worse, and I encouraged her to see her doctor for a reevaluation.

One day I asked her if she wanted to try an experiment that might help her. I taught her Heart-Centered Meditation, which follows, and she was immediately able to feel and rest into the energy of unconditional love.

The following meditation is practiced throughout the world in many traditions. It is based on the belief that living through or meditating on the heart center brings us and others into harmony, balance, and unconditional love. It is an example of a focused meditation. Do not be deceived by its apparent simplicity—when practiced with dedication, it produces powerful results. You may want to use a timer to signal the end of the meditation after ten to twenty minutes, gradually increasing to longer periods.

Exercise: Heart-Centered Meditation

1. Find a quiet place. Sit in a comfortable position. Close your eyes. Relax your jaw, shoulders, and belly.

2. Take a few deep breaths and release any tension in your body.

3. Place your hands on your heart center, the energy center in the middle of your chest.

4. Imagine that your heart center is a crystal chalice, ready to receive healing and transforming energy from God, Mother Nature, Allah, Source, Universal Energy, the Good, Krishna, or your Higher Power—whatever you call the Transcendent.

5. Connect to that source. Visualize the pristine light and energy that flows from the source directly into your heart. Your heart center will open easily to receive this unconditional love, the pure love that accepts you totally as you are and requires nothing in return.

6. Keep all your attention on your heart center. If your attention wanders, gently bring it back. You may feel a warmth or tingling in the area. Stay gently focused here as long as you wish, and you will open even more to receive unconditional love from the source.

7. After a while you'll feel the energy overflowing the chalice, bubbling from your heart center into all parts of your body. Your mind will be peaceful, and sometimes blissful.

8. Know that the energy of unconditional love transforms, balances, and heals every cell, tissue, organ, bone, and fluid in your body. It calms your bodymind and washes away tensions and energies, which are no longer needed.

9. When you feel full and peaceful, direct the energy from your heart to people you know, as well as those

you don't. See and feel the light traveling from your heart to theirs. Thinking their names will help you connect to them. In this way you also may bless animals, trees, the environment, governments, events— anything you wish.

10. End your meditation with a statement or gesture of gratitude for the privilege of having this experience. I place my palms together, bow my head, and think of a statement like, "I give thanks," or "I'm grateful for the grace of this moment."

Mitsuko practiced the meditation every day and reported that it brought her great relief and lifted her out of her fears, and that she'd had fewer panic attacks since she had begun the practice. And with her new sense of having some control over her disabling episodes, she felt motivated to take her medication. By practicing unconditional love, she was moving toward wholeness.

The attribute of compassion is a natural companion to unconditional love. A compassionate heart feels no separation between self and other, is able to feel along with another person (which is different than having pity or sympathy), and can take love into action to help that person. Having compassion for someone means you wish that being to be free from suffering.

If you are facing death or are seriously ill, practicing the Heart-Centered Meditation is the most valuable thing you can do for yourself and others. Once you are able to enter unconditional love at will, you have a means of lifting yourself out of emotional and, sometimes, physical pain. You will have more joy and peace, even in the midst of the chaos of illness. It is an energy that is beautifully contagious, so those around you will receive its blessing. When you become unconditional love, you claim and share the spiritual heritage that belongs to every human being. Many spiritual texts emphasize that when we meditate on agape, unconditional love, and compassion, we are adding to the collective experience, sharing it with everyone on earth.

As Elisabeth Kübler-Ross, a pioneer in the field of death and dying, said, "The ultimate lesson all of us have to learn is unconditional love, which includes not only others but ourselves as well."

CHAPTER 6

Be Present

Death is not extinguishing the light; it is only putting out the lamp because the dawn has come.

—Rabindranath Tagore

When people first learn they have a life-limiting illness, they often either retreat into themselves or want to engage the world even more. The first response is a helpful phase, a time of reflection and planning, of making health care decisions, and of cutting away unessential involvements with others and less meaningful activities. It's a time of gathering one's energies and resources. The second response also is useful—to do what is meaningful while one is still physically able.

I have a friend with untreatable cancer who is busily traveling through Europe, visiting all the vineyards and gourmet restaurants while she still is able to taste great wines and gourmet meals, and a client at the end of life who doesn't want to see anyone except his wife. Desire for inward retraction or outward expansion are both healthy movements in consciousness during severe illness. Pay attention to these rhythms of being drawn inward or nudged outward, and follow them, because they correspond to rhythms in the body. Your body needs times of activity and times of rest to maximize healing potential and minimize discomfort, and you can tune in to yourself to feel what level of activity is appropriate at any given time.

Being present in your life is something different; it has little to do with the expansion-contraction rhythms described. It means *you do not disappear into your illness*. When we stay present we are awake to our challenges, no matter how great the pain or fear. Even when we are in a black hole of suffering and have to ask others to make decisions for us, there is some part of us that is present and feels and knows we are ultimately in charge of our own lives, no matter what is happening.

We are in touch with an inner guiding principle, no matter how tough the medical treatment or pain is. No matter how "out of it" we may be, some part is still witnessing everything. This part can communicate clearly when necessary. When we are present during illness, our experiences are richer and more meaningful, no matter what our condition. And when it's time to surrender to death, we can choose to be present by making our own choices and showing up for all the unfolding mystery of the dying experience.

People with illness who are not present in their lives may be caught in a victim state. They are disinterested in the quality of their lives, and have given up their power to make choices. They don't care what treatments their physicians offer and won't guide family members in end-of-life decisions. They don't care whether they live or die. I'm not referring to those who may be severely depressed or semiconscious, but to those who have decided they have been given a raw deal and who rebel against working with their situation. In any case, for as long as possible, it's meaningful to be present in order to make wise choices at the end of your life.

The following exercise will initiate a meaningful inquiry into being present.

Exercise: Expansion, Contraction, or Balance?

Take out your journal and write about how you are experiencing the rhythms of your life. Address these questions and add whatever comes to mind about keeping your life big. Accept what you discover without judgment.

1. Is there anywhere in my life I'm hiding, giving up, or disappearing into my illness?

2. When do I feel most alive, most fully myself?

3. Are there areas of my life where I want to be more present?

4. Are there times in my life—perhaps during medical procedures—when it's appropriate not to be aware and present?

5. Do I feel a balance in the amount of time I'm in expansive states, neutral states, and contractive states?

6. What do I feel about the idea of being present for my own death?

There are no correct answers to these questions. You are exploring your rhythms of awareness in your life now, and noticing how, when, and where you are present. You have the right to make these choices, and it's healthier to make *conscious* choices about what you are doing, rather than falling into automatic behavior.

After you have finished the exercise, contemplate what you've written. Make a list of areas of your life where you want to make changes to become more present instead of disappearing or giving up. Write down the names of people with whom you intend to be more present. Refer back to these writings at least once a week. Practice.

⌒

Many years ago, I learned how difficult it is for some people to live in the present moment from a client of mine. Abdullah was thirty-one years old. He had end-stage heart disease, and since his diagnosis he had suffered from constant anxiety and panic attacks. The medication he took to alleviate his anxiety did not completely control his problem, so his physician referred him to me for stress management. Abdullah said he had been a "worrier" his whole life, always thinking about what could go wrong in a situation and juggling various solutions to these imagined problems. He was caught in his mind with these musings, distracted from what he was actually doing in the moment, and often not remembering what he had been involved with an hour earlier.

He did not understand the concept of having his total attention on whatever he was doing—concentrating on the action of washing the dishes as he cleaned plates at the sink, or noticing his various sensations as he mowed the lawn—instead of obsessing about other things. Abdullah believed he had more control of his life if he anticipated everything that could go wrong. I said the reverse was true, that when we are present, we have a clear mind and can make good decisions easily and quickly. To illustrate "living in the now," I told him this ancient Taoist fable.

Once a monk was strolling in the forest. He was enjoying the scent of the spring air and the colors of the flowers and foliage. Suddenly he heard growling behind him, and when he turned around, he saw a large tiger following him. He started to run, at the same time chanting prayers to calm the tiger. But the tiger began running after him, growling fiercely. They ran and ran, the monk's leather sandals flapping and slapping so loudly that the birds flew off the trees.

When he was almost out of breath, the monk came to a cliff and slid over the edge, catching a protruding blackberry shrub several feet below. He was holding on with one hand. There were thorns on the branches, but the monk held steady and calmed himself. He looked up at the tiger that was trying to get him from above, and when he looked below at the bottom of the cliff, he was shocked to see another tiger lying in wait. He didn't know what to do.

The monk sighed deeply and looked to the side, where he saw a large, plump berry at the end of one branch. He smiled. And even though the thorns dug into the hand that secured him to the bush, he stretched his other arm out and plucked the berry. The scent of that blackberry made him happy, and its globules glistened, promising him sweetness. He bit into it and chewed it slowly, enjoying its juiciness and texture. It was the best berry he had ever eaten.

Abdullah and I talked about the meaning of the story. The tiger above is our past, which pursues our attention; the tiger below is the future that awaits us. Our challenge is to move away from the past and the future and to live in the present. Even though the present may sting, like the thorns on the bush, it is the place where life bears fruit.

He said, "But the monk will die anyway . . . so what's the point?"

"That is the point," I replied. "Everything dies, so all we have is now." When we realize this and keep our attention, thoughts, and actions oriented to present time, time slows down, and we can go more deeply into our experiences. Then we live our lives from a more centered perspective, and each moment, day, and year becomes fuller and more satisfying.

I'm happy to report that after several months of working together Abdullah did learn to experience being present. He told me he was not so afraid of death anymore. Although he'd had a frustrating beginning, he came to enjoy the practices I gave him, and his anxiety was considerably reduced. Here's one he practiced with enthusiasm.

Exercise: Right Here, Right Now

1. Get a watch or cell phone that has a timer or alarm function.

2. Set the alarm to ring four hours from now. If you know you'll be in a meeting or driving at that time, it's okay to make it a bit later.

3. When the alarm rings at the appointed time, sit down in a comfortable place where you won't be disturbed. If there are other people around, you still may be able

to do the exercise. A client of mine excuses herself and steps outside her office building.

4. Close your eyes and take six or seven deep breaths, exhaling slowly.

5. Look around at your environment for a few minutes, noticing the details of everything you see. Keep your attention on what you are doing. If your mind wanders, bring it back.

6. Close your eyes and notice the sensations in your body: tension in the shoulders, cold hands, tingling or energy in your legs, warm belly, etc. What part of your body is the most relaxed? The most tense? Then take some deep breaths to release any tension.

7. Ask yourself what you are feeling in this moment. Happy, neutral, sleepy, angry, etc. Try not to drift into thought about your emotions—just focus on the feelings themselves. Keep all your attention on the feelings for a few moments, without trying to change them.

8. Center in your heart for a few minutes, as you learned to do in chapter five. Breathe deeply and open your eyes.

9. Reset the alarm for four hours from now, and repeat this exercise when it rings.

10. After you have practiced for a week at four-hour intervals during the time you are awake, experiment with doing the exercise every three hours. When you are able, try checking in at one-hour intervals for a day.

As you become more skilled at this exercise, you'll find your-self checking in with your environment, body, and feelings easily. Soon you can eliminate the timer altogether and you will have developed the ability to be present no matter where you are. Then you can practice being present with another person, by having relaxed attention on what he or she is saying and doing. This is the basis of active listening.

CHAPTER 7

Living with Discomfort

Since we're all going to die, it's obvious that when
and how don't matter.

—Albert Camus, *The Stranger*

The dictionary has a plethora of words to describe discomfort: *ache, soreness, tenderness, irritation, stiffness, twinge, throb, pang, cramp,* and *pain.* Also part of the definition are: *inconvenience, difficulty, bother, nuisance, vexation, drawback, disadvantage, trouble, problem, trial, tribulation, hardship,* and *hassle.* Those of you with a life-limiting illness have, I'm sure, experienced many—if not all—of these states of discomfort. It's truly amazing how our bodies can express themselves when things are not going well.

All illness has components of discomfort, and when the illness is serious, pain is usually present. We all fear pain. We know it can take over and consume our attention so much that we don't feel like ourselves anymore, but like we're trapped in a cage of horrible sensations that make us want to scream. Continual pain wears us down. Pain management is recognized as such an important part of patient care that there are organizations of researchers and physician specialists in the field of pain medicine. They have a varied armamentarium to reduce chronic pain, such as biofeedback, hypnosis, nerve block injections, and electrical stimulators. You can ask your physician for a referral to a pain specialist if necessary. There also have been studies that show pet therapy is a great pain reliever, as are quality sleep and gentle stretching exercises, like yoga or tai chi. Mindfulness meditation is being used to successfully alleviate pain and discomfort. And healthy nutrition and managing stress also are important in becoming free from pain.

There is a difference between pain—a physical sensation—and suffering, which is how we experience the pain in an emotionally distressing way. We also can suffer over psychological matters that are distressing us, such as knowing that our lives will come to an end. What's interesting is that what one person suffers with may not cause suffering for another. Attitudes, beliefs, our perceptions, and where we place our attention during episodes of pain or suffering greatly influence our experience, and with training, we can learn to modify our response.

We have the ability to change, lessen, or even eliminate our response to pain and suffering by engaging the practices of mind-body medicine. And here I'm using the term *medicine*, as the Native Americans and other indigenous people use it: a natural, powerful healing agent. Hippocrates said that the natural healing force within us is the means to getting well. Ancient healing practices such as yoga, ayurvedic medicine, traditional Chinese medicine, and shamanic healing in tribes all over the world subscribe to the view that the mind and body are one. The mind can not only influence physical health but is the key to all healing. In this chapter we'll be focusing on how to use our minds to alter our experience of pain and suffering.

Don't push to control

One of the things that can cause physical discomfort and pain is our need to control. If you tense up and begin to resist pain or discomfort the minute you have it, the symptoms will get worse. This increases muscle tension, heart rate, and blood pressure, and activates even more biochemical output. We are on alert, hypervigilant, focused on the pain, and looking for a hint of any more pain that might be waiting to pounce on us. We become so attentive to the expectation of pain that it takes over our whole experience. It's not that we don't do our best to heal, but that we should let go of the expectation and need to be completely pain-free before living an enjoyable life. You may not realize how much you have linked your mood to physical sensations, and how that can change. We are much more than emotion/sensation, and there is a depth of peace beyond that.

Instead of getting caught in an automatic activation in response to pain or discomfort, we can learn to calm or switch off the response entirely. With practice, we can prepare a strategy to use at the first sign of pain that will change the automatic activating response. It's done with mind-body medicine. As an example consider a client of mine, Julia, who had bone cancer and experienced so much pain consistently that she finally had to quit her job. The medications she was taking did help, but they also were difficult for her to swallow and made her groggy. She practiced meditation and the following exercise, and soon was able to reduce her pain and other symptoms of discomfort significantly.

Exercise: The Shuttle

This mind-body practice is simple in concept, but powerful in its ability to ameliorate discomfort. The principle is that a person learns that her mind can influence and change her perception of pain, itching, numbness, tingling, and other symptoms. It is a form of hypnotic analgesia called the Shuttle. I have found that in conjunction with medication or as a first line of treatment this exercise can provide relief from even the most severe symptoms. In some, it is also helpful in disengaging from obsessive thoughts.

1. Choose a sound in your environment. It can be the singing of birds, the loud tick of a clock, a refrigerator hum, or a soothing piece of music that is playing. This sound is your ally, your helper.

2. Lie down if you can, or find another position in which you feel relaxed. Focus your attention on the area of your body that is symptomatic. If it's pain, notice what kind of pain it is—sharp, constant aching, or an intermittent dull pressure, or something else. Notice the area the pain encompasses.

3. Now allow yourself to feel the pain totally. Surrender to the pain without resistance. Relax into it. Place all your attention on the pain and keep it there for at least a minute or two.

4. Switch your attention to your ally. Listen to the sound without thinking about it. Hear it with all your attention. Imagine you are hearing birds for the first time, that the sound is a revelation, entirely new. Focus for a few minutes on the sound.

5. Switch back to your bodily pain. Again, place all your attention on the pain. You may notice that it has changed; perhaps it's less intense. Stay with the area of the pain for a few minutes.

6. Shuttle back to your ally again. Listen with full attention for several minutes. Then shuttle to the pain area again.

7. Continue shuttling between the pain and your ally. It may take only a few times or as many as eight or nine. Eventually, you will notice that the pain is greatly diminished or, in many cases, that you can't find the pain anymore.

8. If someone is helping you with this method, he or she can provide a pleasant sound. I ring a small bell for the ally. Some people need to keep their attention on the pain and sound for more than a few minutes, so repeat the exercise with longer intervals if necessary.

9. Remember, the more you practice this exercise, the more skilled you will become in rapidly reducing your pain level.

You can also figure out what little things bring you comfort—ice water, sitting up versus lying down, quiet music, being alone or with others, etc. Be prepared! I had a friend who was near death who had sudden episodes of sweating and hot flashes. With a yell, she would order her family out of the room, shouting, "It's coming!" She then would ask me to undress her so she could lie nude with arms and legs outstretched. Then she would sigh with relief and begin conversing. Whatever it takes, claim the right to make yourself comfortable.

Practice mind-body medicine

I'll tell you about a friend of mine who was present with her illness and received relief from pain by practicing the techniques in this chapter.

I had known Emma for about twenty years when I got the call. She was ninety years old.

"I can't come to the May workshop, Carolyn, because I've got cancer." She had been experiencing pain in her abdomen for months, and her physician had treated her for irritable bowel syndrome, which didn't alleviate the pain. Body scans had not identified any problem, so then she received medication for anxiety.

But she still had pain, which kept her from enjoying her usual activities. After a few weeks of Emma lying on the couch clutching her abdomen in distress, her physician referred her for exploratory surgery, which showed she had cancer in her stomach and bowel to such an extent that the surgeon could do nothing. Her doctor told her she had only a few months to live, and promised to keep her comfortable.

Emma Rose, as she always introduced herself, had been a dramatic actress, and she still traveled, went to concerts and lectures, and enjoyed socializing, particularly when martinis were involved. She dated several men, complaining that they were too worn out for sex. She lived alone in a modern senior complex that encouraged independence, and independent she was! She loved to race down the halls in her electric scooter wearing a flamboyant dress and a white cowboy hat, and was reprimanded several times for speeding. Emma attended at least five of my seminars around the country each year. When she was eighty-five, she came to my weeklong retreat in the Turks and Caicos Islands, where she ripped off her clothes and dove into the ocean to convince the twenty participants that nude bathing was healthy. What a fun character she was.

Emma addressed her impending death with the same verve as she had lived her life. "I've gone into high gear," she told me on the phone. "I've changed my will and gotten a do not resuscitate order put on my health care directive, and made a list of all my belongings and who they go to—you get my mother's painting—and I've located an agency with part-time helpers for later so I can die at home, and, well, I think everything is taken care of." She was talking and breathing fast, but her voice was matter-of-fact.

I have never worked with anyone who was as prepared for death as Emma. The envelope containing the document "In Case of My Death," which she had always carried in her purse since age twenty, certainly illustrated her commitment to attending to her own mortality. I had seen an iteration of this envelope at every retreat she attended, since she propped it up on a desk in her room and reminded me that it was there. It contained fastidious instructions regarding her lawyer, prepaid funeral, and her wishes not to have a service of any kind or a viewing of her body. She named who would attend to the arrangements. She wanted to be responsible until the last minute, and didn't want to burden anyone.

In this sense, Emma's practical attitude about her own death allowed her to face it head-on even in the final difficult moments, as though she had been granted a golden sword with which to cut a path through the dark forest, with vigor and efficiency. She was entirely unsentimental about the fact that all life on earth ends, and felt it was her time to go so younger life could blossom. Often when she brought this up we had discussed how difficult it is for most people to deal with the ending of a life cycle and the underlying principle of all nature: The old must die in order for the new to be born.

She was cooperative with her physician and took the pain medication he prescribed, but liked to have periods of time off her meds so she was more clear-minded. She knew that being open to new mind-body methodologies would help her to keep her life big. Emma wanted to try all my techniques for pain reduction, and received consistent relief from the following two.

Exercise: Talk to Your Pain

In this exercise we use our imagination to create a relationship with the pain. We can't heal or modify that which we don't know. Rather than seeing the pain as an enemy, in this exercise we open to understanding what the pain wants to tell us about itself and ourselves. Hidden psychological dynamics are revealed in this dialogue, and something positive happens physically when we move into the pain instead of pushing it away.

1. Have your journal, a pad of paper, and crayons or felt-tip pens nearby, and a pen to write with.

2. Sit comfortably and close your eyes. Take seven deep belly breaths, breathing through your nose only. Imagine that you are inhaling air all the way down into your belly, and as you inhale, allow your lower abdomen to

expand fully. Then let out your breath as slowly as you can. Relax your jaw, shoulders, and belly.

3. Place your attention on the area of pain. Ask your inner wisdom to present you with an image of what the pain looks like. Accept whatever comes, no matter how illogical.

4. Pick up the crayons and draw the image. Then draw an abstract picture of what the pain feels like on another page.

5. Take a moment to look at each drawing.

6. Pick up your journal and pen and write: *What do you want to tell me? What's going on in there?*

7. Without thinking, write the words coming into your mind that are the response to your question. It might look like this: *I'm red hot and angry. I've been here for a long time, but you are just noticing me. I've been burning up for a long time.*

8. Ask your pain another question; continue the dialogue back and forth. You might ask: *Why are you angry? What about?* Continue dialoguing for at least a page. Remember, let anything at all come into your mind for writing.

9. Read what you have written. Accept this first dialogue as truth in the moment, even if it seems illogical. You can go back to the dialogue on another day and ask new questions, such as: *What do you need to be healed?*

10. When you have finished your dialogue, place your hands over the area of pain. Take a deep breath and relax. Thank your inner wisdom for providing you with valuable information.

After you've completed your dialogue with your pain, you can segue into this next exercise. Or you can use it alone at any time. I teach it to all my clients who are dealing with pain as well as those who aren't. I've found that children are especially gifted in doing energy medicine, so get into the mind-set of a trusting child who values the imagination.

Exercise: Energy Medicine for Pain

Children know that when they are hurt, the best remedy is Mom's touch. And Mother knows that when she places a hand on her child's bruised leg or bumped head, the area is soothed and the child is comforted. We learned about energy medicine in chapter two, so you already have some of these skills. This exercise involves focused use of energy, instead of having it flow through your body.

1. Center yourself with a few deep breaths and close your eyes.

2. Connect to Source, God, Universal Mind, unconditional love, etc.

3. Visualize light and energy pouring onto the top of your head, where it forms a beautiful ball of spinning light, and keep all your attention on the light.

4. Let the ball of light flow easily through the core of your body to your heart center, where it forms a second spinning ball of light. Hold your attention here for a minute or so. Open even more to unconditional love, Divinity.

5. Direct the light from your heart up to your shoulders, down your arms, and to your hands, which are each surrounded with balls of light.

6. Notice the orbs of light at your head, heart, and hands. The energy is flowing easily and is abundant.

7. Place your hands on the part of your body where you are having pain. Again, connect to your transpersonal source and open to the flow of healing energy. Open and receive the energy.

8. Keep your attention on the area of pain and the energy flowing into this place. Breathe fully and normally. Let go of any tension in your shoulders, jaw, and belly.

9. You'll find that the pain soon begins to subside, but keep directing the energy flow for as long as twenty minutes. Relax and enjoy the experience. You'll sense when to stop.

If you can't reach the area of pain with your hands, go through all the steps, but instead of doing number 7 in the exercise, *visualize* the energy circulating. See the light penetrating deep into the tissue, knowing that the energy transforms and soothes the area, which reduces pain. Practice this technique so you'll have it available when you need it. You can also use focused energy medicine to help others—just place your hands on them where it hurts and bring in the light. Don't be shy about teaching this to family and friends—it's wonderful to participate in a group healing in this way, whether you are the healers or the recipient. Everyone merges into a unified experience of healing energy and unconditional love. It is a state of being without an object, an experience that brings everyone into wholeness.

Surround yourself with nourishing people

There's nothing worse than being sick and trying to come to terms with your own death only to have the people around you push their own agendas about what you should do. No matter how well-meaning family and friends may be, their anxiety and discomfort with the idea of their own death can throw them into states of mind that can be annoying and destructive to your well-being. When ill people have psychological discomfort, it increases their physical discomfort. I'll give you the example of a young client of mine named Hailey, who had been bedridden for several months with metastatic melanoma. She had no family, but the staff at the newspaper where she had been a reporter had supported her by visiting daily. They brought flowers and books, discussed the news with her, and tried to entertain her with jokes and funny stories.

She appreciated their care, but when she was finally hospitalized for the two weeks before her death, she'd had enough. "It's too much," she told me. "I can't wait until they leave, because now that they're accepting the truth—that I'll be gone soon—each one is insisting I try some homeopathic remedy or something. They're intense. They leave all this stuff and I don't want to lie and say I've used it. I just want to be left alone in peace. And you know what? When they're here, my body hurts more."

Hailey told me she was embarrassed to say that she didn't want any of her office friends to visit. She said she was content with my visits, and enjoyed the poetry I read her and the meditating we did together. She assured me this was enough. I suggested that she could talk to her friends about what they were doing and ask them to support her in the ways she wanted, but she didn't trust that they could change. I was there when she told her group of friends that this was the time to say good-bye—she needed to be alone for the rest of her journey.

Hailey teaches us to take charge of our social environment. Choose the people you want to be with while you are dealing with life-and-death decisions. Limit the time you spend with them to suit you, and speak up about what is helpful and what you don't want to hear. Again, it's all about keeping your life big. Don't let anyone wear you down so you lose your dignity and collapse into them.

Explore stillness

Our whole world changes for the better when we can learn to appreciate stillness. Creating stillness can be daunting, because we can't rely on our usual busyness to occupy our minds. Whether it's through meditation, being in nature, or just sitting quietly at home, cultivating a quiet mind and body is healing and brings us into our wholeness. Our mind, brain, and body synchronize and work together harmoniously. Stillness creates spaciousness. It is part of the natural cycle of contraction that we discussed earlier, in contrast to the activating phases.

Stillness is more than silence. Although silence is helpful in achieving stillness, we can find and actually *become* stillness in the middle of a cheering crowd. We also can experience inner stillness while dancing or swimming laps. When we connect deeply to our innermost core that is neither thought nor feeling, we become the pure awareness that is the ground of our being. It is a place of peace that underlies all mental and physical activity. Here there is no pain, no illness, no concerns, no thought, no emotion. There is only awareness. We are most alive when centered in our stillness. And we are truly home.

When you are in pain, it's important to become still.

Exercise: Become Stillness

1. Sit or lie down in a comfortable position, keeping your body relaxed. Let the bed or chair support you; feel yourself sinking into the furniture.

2. Close your eyes; take a few deep breaths and let them out slowly. Then breathe normally.

3. Notice the space between your thoughts. Allow the spaces to become larger and longer. With practice, you can achieve a period of spaciousness with very little thought.

4. Stay this way as long as you wish. Be as calm and quiet as the surface of a still pond on a summer afternoon. When you finish, you'll notice that your psychological or physical pain or discomfort has changed for the better.

Be fluid with change

Just as our mental and physical energies are always moving between states of expansion and contraction, or activity and rest, the world around us, and in fact the whole universe, is doing the same. Everything changes. In every moment, everything is changing in some way. I like the line from the movie *Phenomenon*, in which the dying protagonist says, "Everything is on its way to somewhere." It's a blessing that we don't usually notice this, or life would seem unstable. When we are ill, we are particularly sensitive and change is even more difficult to handle. A change in medical routine, in our environment, or even in a blood test result can seem like a catastrophe. When we are doing our best to manage our emotions and stay as healthy as possible for the time we have left to live, change can feel threatening.

To keep ourselves comfortable, we need an open attitude about change. We need to accept that it happens and may be beyond our control. The solution is to reach deep into the core of our being, the place of peace that is untouched by change, and rest into its spaciousness. From here, whatever happens externally will not be experienced as a threat. This doesn't mean that we become passive; to the contrary, by being fluid with change and coming from our essence we are better equipped to clearly make decisions and ask for what we need. It also helps us accept that death is natural, and that we too will be experiencing a mystical transformation from form to nonform.

There is a Zen story that epitomizes someone who is fluid with change. It goes like this:

> Once there was a wise old monk who lived alone in a
> little house on the side of a mountain. People came to
> him for healing and advice about problems in their
> lives. He was well respected by the villagers.

An irate man showed up one day with his daughter, who was carrying a baby. The girl falsely accused the monk of getting her pregnant. The angry father told the monk he was responsible for raising the child. The monk replied only, "Ah, so." He accepted the child and raised her as his own, teaching her meditation and the healing arts. His home was filled with the joy and love between them.

Years later, the mother came back and demanded that her child return to live with her in order to work in the fields. The monk looked into the eyes of the child with love, giving her courage and hope to carry on. Then he turned to the mother, bowed, and said, "Ah, so."

You may think the monk was too passive and should have stood up for himself. We certainly can have compassion for his sacrifice in taking on the responsibility of a baby, and again when the child he had come to love was wrenched from his life. The point of the story is that it's possible to adjust to any change, no matter how difficult, if we are connected to our inner center, which is changeless and flows with the life around us.

To be or not to be

As Emma's health deteriorated even more, she became very philosophical and questioned basic issues that most people with terminal illness have considered: Should I take my own life before I enter a phase of intolerable suffering? Can I reduce the burden of my suffering on my loved ones by accelerating my demise? She admired the people in Oregon and Washington who had chosen physician-assisted suicide, which is legal there, and though the option wasn't available in her state, she wanted to think about it. She wanted to be in charge of her exit.

Our discussions ranged from the moral/legal aspects of suicide to religious concerns. When she questioned how tribal societies view suicide when someone is debilitated, I told her about the Chukchi tribes in the Arctic and eastern Russia. Ethnographic records reveal that before government regulation, these people practiced a form of suicide when they became old or feeble. The Siberian Chukchi would determine through prayer and ritual the correct timing of his own death, and would ask a family member to kill him. After being asked three times, the relative was obligated to carry out the request, usually with a knife or gun. Although the act was a personal surrender to the inevitability of aging and disease, as well as relieving the villagers of the burden of a nonfunctional member, it also was done as a sacrifice to the ancestors, giving them the energy of the departed one. The person requesting death was honored as a warrior because of his choice. Of course, it's illegal now, but when it was practiced, it was because the Chukchi felt it was their time to rejoin their ancestors in the other life, and to relieve the tribe of the responsibility of their care. To them it was a continuation of life in another form, since no one and nothing in nature ever truly died. As spirits, they still would be attuned to their families in the village, helping and guiding them. The connection of their human existence to the spirit world was solid, with each world helping and nourishing the other.

Emma asked me if I would choose when to end my life if I were terminally ill, and I told her that I preferred to have the experience of going through the dying process naturally, that probably there's something to learn in the liminal stage between life and death; however, I did want to maintain my awareness and dignity. I told her I trusted that I would know what to do when the time came if I were terminal and suffering excessively. As we ended our discussion, she said she thought the Chukchi had it right, but that she would choose the natural exit.

The issue of suicide to end suffering is a deeply personal matter, influenced by cultural and religious values. It's related to another end-of-life issue: quality of life. It's normal to think about taking charge of your own death when you are terminally ill and suffering, so no one needs to feel ashamed about it.

Today, when offering treatment choices it is common for physicians to talk about quality of life with their patients who have a terminal illness. Thankfully, more medical professionals are seeking training in the field of end-of-life care than ever before.

Let me go, please

Another common problem that presents itself at the end of life comes in the form of relatives who won't let a loved one go. Recently I visited a woman in the hospital who had undergone three difficult rounds of chemotherapy and radiation for a devastating cancer. She was ninety-three years old and felt complete with her life. Her family badgered her to do another round of chemo, to the point they wore her down and she acquiesced to please them. She was devastated at the prospect of "revving up my life" when the treatment would probably extend her life only a few months. "Can't I just lie here peacefully and look out the window and wonder what comes after death?" she asked me.

If you are in this position, take courage and claim your power to make your own decisions about the final phase of your life. You have the right to refuse treatment, to do what is right for you, and your family's ideas about treatment or how you should die are not as important as your own wishes. Even if they are hurt by your decision to choose a natural demise without life-extending methods, trust that they will learn how to handle their distress. Completing your life the way you wish is paramount.

If a discussion like this with your family seems too difficult for you to do by yourself, arrange to have them come together for a meeting with a trusted friend, minister, therapist, or social worker to facilitate you and your loved ones in a heart-to-heart exchange. Or you could begin by consulting with a hospice worker—all have experience in these areas and are available to help you weigh your options.

When you have made your decisions, call the family together. Start by clearly listing your specific wishes about whether you have chosen to accept or refuse further treatment, how you want to spend your remaining time, what you need from those present, what you want during your last days or hours, how you would like your body treated after your death, and details about a memorial or funeral if you want one. After you have announced your wishes, family members have their chance to share how they feel about this with you. Let each express concerns or comments, but be strong in stating what you have decided. Remember, it is your life. Again, one of the best resources for helping you explore these issues before discussing them with your family is hospice.

Hospice

In the United States, the National Hospice and Palliative Care Organization has grown to be a significant part of the health care system, with more than five thousand programs and most private health insurances and Medicare paying for their services. Their website has a multitude of resources. Hospice care also is available in nursing homes, prisons, veterans' facilities, and hospitals. Ask your physician to prescribe hospice; then you are eligible to have an initial consultation with someone from a service provider. Knowing the facts and procedures before you or a loved one needs hospice care is valuable.

I have met volunteers from these organizations, and I admire the depth of their training and their dedication to helping people face death. With the increase in our aging population and our changing medical and ethical values regarding the dying, there will be more end-of-life organizations like these that will open their doors to the dying. Rather than being rushed to the hospital in the final stage of death, the terminally ill person can choose to die at home with twenty-four-hour hospice support or go to a homelike hospice facility where compassionate caregivers provide medical and emotional support.

The ending of each life is unique

Four months after Emma's diagnosis, our phone conversations began to happen less frequently, because when I called, Iris, the helper she had hired, said she was sleeping. I checked with her lawyer, her chosen advocate to manage her final care, who reported that her pain had increased and large morphine doses kept her sleeping most of the day. When I did talk with her, she asked me to come visit her, saying that although she had beat the doctor's prediction of death in two months, she felt her time was near. I wanted to be with my friend one more time, so I traveled out to meet her.

"Is there anything I can do for you?" I asked as I held her hand.

"You can get Iris to bring mouthwash, 'cause I don't want bad breath," she mumbled. With a nurse from the clinic coming three times a day, Iris had become Emma's caretaker, even staying overnight in a cot next to her bed. Iris said she was very devoted to "*la señora*" and had cared for her like she did her own mother. The nursing staff assured me they had arranged for hospice to take over the next day.

I slept on the couch and went to her several times during the night. She was restless, but sleeping. A phrase kept repeating in my mind: "Life is magnificently fragile." The phrase had occurred to me as a child; I would ponder it and then forget it for a few years, then it would enter my awareness again, with a deep feeling of awe. Something magical is happening, I thought. The human passage from form to nonform. Our minds can't fully understand death, but we are invited to embrace it.

A male nurse from hospice arrived the next morning with bedside supplies and medications. Emma woke up and watched quietly. If she weren't ill, she would have told him he was handsome and that she liked dark men, I thought. I showed him around the condo and told Iris she could go home. She touched Emma on the shoulder and sweetly said a prayer in Spanish, then kissed her on the forehead. As she walked to the door, she was crying.

Emma had not spoken a word. She seemed alert and her eyes were open.

"Say something," she whispered. I knew she didn't mean conversation. In the workshops she had attended, we had explored chants and prayers from many religions. She had enjoyed them all.

"I'll do the Green Tara chant, a blessing to end suffering and bring whatever a person needs. Is that all right?" She nodded.

"Om Tara tutare ture svaha," I chanted softly over and over. I felt a deep peace surround us. After a few minutes, she whispered to me, so I stopped and bent down to listen.

"I love you," she said.

"I love you too, Emma."

She closed her eyes and fell asleep.

For two days she continued to sleep through the change of nurses and their ministrations. I sat in her room and meditated several times a day, and read and went to the gym or the building café. Her lawyer came over to say good-bye and to coordinate funeral arrangements with hospice.

That night the nurse woke me. "Emma is taking her final breaths," she said.

I leaned close to her and said, "I am here, Emma. Right here.

You are entering love; open to it. Love surrounds you; open to it. Let go into love." And she did.

In this chapter you have learned several techniques to manage pain and discomfort. You have seen through Emma's story how one person faced death in a matter-of-fact way, viewing her own demise as a natural conclusion to a life well lived. I invite you to practice these exercises now, so you will be able to do them easily when you need relief from pain or discomfort.

CHAPTER 8

Practice Forgiveness

Death must be so beautiful. To lie in the soft brown earth, with the grasses waving above one's head, and listen to silence. To have no yesterday, and no tomorrow. To forget time, to forgive life, to be at peace.

—Oscar Wilde, *The Canterville Ghost*

For all the people I've worked with who knew they were dying, it was vitally important to seek forgiveness for their misdeeds. They not only wanted to soothe their own conscience, but they genuinely felt a desire to create harmony and set the injured person free from the harm that had been done. It didn't matter if the incident was a small one and long forgotten—most of my clients have felt a strong urge to receive the blessing of being forgiven. And the reverse has also been true—they felt a need to seek out the people who had harmed them, and to offer forgiveness. We have built into us a striving for closure, and healing relationships that are out of balance is a primary factor. These needs come from the heart and represent a natural movement toward wholeness.

Our yearning for forgiveness

Several years ago I received a phone call from Israel saying that one of my friends was dying and wanted to talk to me. It was urgent, the person said. Her failing health, conflicting time zones, and other events made the conversation impossible for a few days. Finally, we connected. She didn't say hello, but immediately blurted out, "I ask forgiveness for anything I have done to hurt you." Her statement startled me, as I thought everything between us was more than fine. She said she was asking for forgiveness from everyone she cared about. She wanted to have a "clean" life before she died. I heard the relief in her voice when I told her there was nothing for me to forgive. It then occurred to me to ask if there was anything I had done to harm her, and if so, if she would forgive me. She explained that she too saw our relationship as harmonious, with nothing to forgive. Our exchange was deeply touching, like an ancient sacred ritual.

I had one client who was consumed with the need to receive forgiveness from his family before he died. Don was forty years old. He had grown up in a small town with hardworking parents and one brother. He had been a maintenance worker at a steel manufacturing plant near Pittsburgh since the age of eighteen, and had no other skills. "It's hard work with those furnaces throwing heat on you all day. Noisy too. But I was good with the machines. I worked rotating shifts, and that's no picnic."

A year earlier in the plant, he was hit by a steel beam, which broke several ribs and vertebrae and damaged both kidneys, so they functioned minimally. "There was insurance money," he said, "so I packed up and moved to California. Haven't been

with my wife and kid because she left me a couple years ago. I
rent a room in this house and it isn't bad—the lady, Dorothy,
doesn't bother me and I pay her to drive me to the doctor and
cook and wash. I watch TV and read westerns."

Don's appearance was skeletal, which made his eyes seem
huge, and his skin had a waxy pallor. Even from four feet away,
I could smell the odor of ammonia coming from his body, a sign
that his kidneys were failing. His speech was slow and method-
ical. He would often interrupt himself to check a pillbox, sip
from a juice bottle, and twice, when the phone rang, he gazed at
it for several rings before answering. He was heavily medicated.

He told me the most important thing in his life was to get
forgiveness from his wife and daughter, whom he had mis-
treated. With explicit detail, Don confessed his unkindness toward them. He said that when drinking beer after work,
sometimes he became very cruel with his words, and "cut them
down to nothing." This went on for many years, and when the
daughter reached puberty, his wife took her child and left. "I
always apologized in the morning," he said, "but I guess that
wasn't enough." He wanted to ask their forgiveness, and hoped
they would be willing to break years of noncommunication. He
had phoned them just before I arrived, but there was no answer.
He had left a message saying he was dying, and he begged them
to call him back.

Even though Don had very little energy and seemed depressed, he was eager to do something to rid himself of the
shame he felt. I gave him a notebook and prompted him to write
down specific acts he was ready to forgive himself for. His list
was long and it was apparent that his inner critic was active in
writing it. He was ashamed not only of the way he had treated

his family but also of things he had done years ago, even as a child. He was carrying a heavy burden.

Don was a Christian, and sprinkled throughout his conversation were biblical quotes. "You know, Jesus forgave the people who put him on the cross," he said absentmindedly. "Even something as terrible as that, he forgave them."

"That's the best example of forgiveness I can think of," I said, and offered him another story—the Celtic myth of Rhiannon. In workshops and private sessions I often employ storytelling, weaving the tale as one might read to a child, in order to put the listener into an altered state where the meta message can be absorbed.

> A long time ago, there was a prince of Wales named Pwyll. He rode in the forest every day on his horse, which was as swift as the wind. One day he saw a beautiful woman in a golden dress, seated on a white horse. They were resting in the shade of a tree. He was mesmerized, and wanted to meet her. Now, this woman was actually a goddess from the heavens, who wanted to marry a mortal man. Her name was Rhiannon, and she was known as the goddess of the moon.
>
> When Pwyll approached her, she yanked the reins of her horse and galloped away so quickly he could not keep up. He was persistent, and the next day when she raced away again, he shouted at her to stop. To his surprise, she did, and when he blurted out that he wanted her for his wife, she said yes.
>
> They were married in Pwyll's castle, becoming king and queen, and had a baby boy. Everyone in the

kingdom was very happy, as was the royal family. But during the celebration of the child's first birthday, the little one disappeared. They searched the castle to no avail. A servant, afraid of being blamed, slaughtered a small animal and put the blood and bones in the mother's bed, announcing that Rhiannon had murdered and eaten her own son. The king was devastated, and believed what he was told.

For her punishment, Rhiannon was fitted with a wooden oxen yoke around her shoulders. She was banished to the outer door of the castle, and whenever a visitor came, she was forced to carry him on her back to the inner rooms of the castle, then turn around and remain outside again to wait for the next visitor. Still grieving the loss of her son and the love of her husband, she carried out her task without complaint for many years. The villagers got used to seeing her outside the castle wall, and by now they admired her dignity and inner strength.

One day a hunter approached the castle with a young man. It was Rhiannon's son, fully grown, and there was no mistaking it—he looked exactly like Pwyll. Rhiannon embraced him and cried. The hunter had found the child in a field near the castle, where a careless servant had left him. He had raised him as his own, and when the boy reached maturity, his resemblance to the king revealed his true identity.

The king was ashamed that he had not believed his wife. He and the people expected a punishment from the queen, because she was the powerful goddess of the moon. But she said she loved her husband and her people and wished them no harm. After that, she was known as the goddess of forgiveness and wisdom. They lived happily ever after.

"That's a good story," Don said when I finished. "To be treated like that—it's hard to believe she would forgive them. That's amazing. Thank you." He said the story gave him hope that no matter how wrong he had been to mistreat his wife and daughter, he could ask for—and perhaps receive—their forgiveness.

"It's just as important for you to forgive yourself," I said. "Let's talk about that."

Self-forgiveness

Don and I discussed the importance of having compassion for ourselves and taking action to forgive ourselves. He listened carefully, but could not accept the idea that he was worthy of self-forgiveness. He questioned the benefit of forgiving himself. I explained that in addition to freeing oneself from a burden of shame that takes tremendous energy, a person who forgives himself is able to be present in life without seeing through filters of guilt. I had facilitated many rituals of forgiveness for students in my workshops, and seen how powerfully they allow a person to be reborn. "My family and God need to forgive me first," he said.

Don wanted to talk more about forgiveness. He was tortured by the fact that his wife and daughter didn't want contact with him. "I must have hurt them really bad," he said.

Don had expended a lot of energy, with more talking than ever. He was yearning for his family's forgiveness. When he assured me he wanted to continue, he shared other things in his life that felt incomplete and needed attention. To me, he had entered the peaceful, elevated state I have witnessed that often precedes death. It appears to be both unconscious acceptance and anticipation. I remember seeing it in my mother in the last days before she died, a quiet, joyful luminosity that shone through her voice, and even through her skin, making it almost transparent. Some part of him knows, I thought. It won't be long now.

He told me he was not ready to do the following meditation when I described it to him. He could not yet take the path of self-forgiveness to peace.

Exercise: Self-Forgiveness Meditation

1. Make a list of the acts you wish to forgive yourself for. Write all the details in your journal.

2. Sit or lie comfortably in a quiet place. Close your eyes and take a few deep breaths to center yourself.

3. Connect to a transpersonal source that has meaning to you: God, Mother Nature, Buddha, Universal Mind, Christ, Mohammad, etc.

4. Envision light and energy and unconditional love coming from the source directly into your heart center, the energy center between your breasts. Place your hands there, one over the other.

5. Open and let yourself be filled with the energy of unconditional love. It has no limits and no judgment. It is the essence of forgiveness. It accepts you as you are. Focus on your heart for a few minutes.

6. One by one, address each act on your list. Say out loud, "I forgive myself for _____. I release this memory. I am purified and healed from it. This is my new beginning."

7. Repeat with each item on your list. It's more powerful to concentrate on addressing just one act per meditation session.

8. Place your attention on the flow of unconditional love coming into your body, mind, and soul. Open to it for as long as you wish.

9. End with a feeling of gratitude for the privilege of being able to forgive yourself.

Another person who felt he couldn't die peacefully until he sought forgiveness was Gerald, from chapter four. With my guidance, he and his son healed their relationship, and a major part of their work was each asking forgiveness of the other. But Gerald also was burdened with several other things he wanted forgiven—cruelly dumping a girlfriend, cheating a friend out of twenty thousand dollars, treating his wife and son poorly, wishing his ex-wife would die, and sometimes not caring about teaching his high school kids well.

There were many more, but the one that bothered Gerald so much that he cried when he told me was the time a neighbor girl saw him outside and brought him a flower from her bouquet. "I feel so ashamed," he said. "I ignored her and waved her off. Her smile changed to hurt. I felt awful and will never forget her look." He decided that he could directly ask the neighbor girl for forgiveness, and his ex-wife also. Both accepted his apologies and told him he was forgiven. As a result, Gerald said he felt "a million pounds lighter and cleansed of shame." For the others, he would do the Self-Forgiveness Meditation. When we do this inner work, not only does it transform us, but I like to think that the energy and healing work travels to the intended recipients, transforming the relationship for both parties through space and time.

Approaching forgiveness

Both Don and Gerald were eager to begin the process of asking for forgiveness, and were willing to deal with the difficulties of facing the people they had harmed. Some wise part of them knew that in order to die in peace, they must set aside any hesitation and begin. But for some, the decision is not so easy. Perhaps you are afraid to trust that the other person will honor your request, or you may even fear that approaching the person will ignite retribution. You may not want to give up your image of innocence regarding the act, or you may feel that you'll lose power in the relationship if you ask for forgiveness. It may also seem like it would be humiliating to admit your mistake. As one client even said to me, "I don't have any reason not to ask; I just *can't*."

All of these feelings are valid, and yet I've seen the positive results of forgiveness work. If you are facing the end of your life, making closure and feeling free from the burden of shame and guilt clears the path to wholeness. There also have been numerous psychological and medical studies investigating the hypothesis that people who have done their forgiveness work are healthier than those who haven't, but overall consistent results haven't been obtained. It continues to be an area of interest to professionals in the health fields, and I am a firm believer in the benefits.

Here is a ritual that will take you into the forgiveness process. Done with sincerity, a ritual changes us. When we put our minds, hearts, and bodies into the experience, the energies shift and we have the opportunity to experience transformation. I find rituals to be very powerful. Although the following ritual is designed for the outdoors, you can modify it for indoors by substituting a lighted candle for the outdoor fire, and by holding the paper over the sink for burning.

Exercise: Forgiveness Ritual

1. Find a place where you can be alone—outside in nature if possible. Have a pad of paper and pen, a pot or bucket, a bottle of water, and matches. Get comfortable in a chair or on the ground.

2. In your journal, write down your intention to forgive. It might be, "I'm ready to forgive [person's name] for the hurt he caused by [specific action]." Or, "I'm ready to forgive myself for [specific action]."

3. Write down why you want to forgive (to free yourself, to have a new beginning, to learn more about love, etc.).

4. Write down how you will behave differently once you have forgiven. For example, you might list: telling the person you have forgiven him, approaching the person with an open heart center, or seeing the person through loving eyes when you meet. List how you will treat yourself once you have forgiven yourself: eliminating self-critical thoughts, reminding yourself that the past is past, amplifying the feeling that you are starting afresh. Write down all thoughts that come to you.

5. Close your eyes and ask your inner wisdom to present you with an image that represents your attainment of forgiveness. It can be a simple image or a complex one. Accept whatever comes, even if it doesn't make sense to you. You may want to draw it in a simple sketch or paint it later.

6. In your own words, write an affirmation showing that you or the other person deserve to be forgiven.

7. Take a separate sheet of paper, and in the middle write the person's name and what needs to be forgiven (number 2). Fold it in half.

8. Call forth a witness to the rest of your ritual. It may be a spiritual being, the trees or wind, the spirit of the earth, or your ancestors—whatever has meaning for you. "I ask that _____ be present to witness my actions." If you have a spiritual practice of prayer, now is the time to pray sincerely.

9. Light a corner of the folded paper and hold it over the bucket. At the last minute, release the burning paper into the empty pot or bucket and watch it burn up. Say to yourself something that indicates you have released the act with forgiveness: "I release my resentments. I

invite love to fill the places where I've been hurt. This is a new beginning."

10. Wash your hands and face with the water for purification and to signal the completion of the ritual. Pour water over the ashes, and dispose of them safely.

11. Place your hands over your heart. Complete the ritual with a feeling of gratitude.

Be open to forgiveness as a spiritual experience

Forgiveness is a spiritual experience. We cry out for it from the depths of our being. Actively entering the forgiveness process can transform us in profound ways. The whole realm of spiritual experience, whether through traditional religion, appreciation of nature, inspirational reading, meditation, being of service, love, yoga, devotion to the arts, etc., is one of life's greatest gifts. Engaging in spiritual pursuits is a necessity for those whose time on earth is limited, because it is the best preparation for completing life and surrendering to death. Spirituality engages the soul.

One of the most beautiful things I've ever experienced was watching a family that I worked with do a Forgiveness Exchange at the father's bedside. It was done with candles placed around his hospital room and the scent of fresh roses in the air. The mother and two adult children wept as they did their part. Everyone knew that it would probably be the last thing they all did together, because the father was dying. Here is the exercise for you to experience.

Exercise: Forgiveness Exchange

When two or more people have been involved in hurting one another, such as a family argument that results in severe criticism of each other, damaging words are often spoken that can't be taken back. It's important to address the issue so there aren't simmering resentments that permanently undermine a friendship or family structure. Hopefully, you have an understanding with the people closest to you, so that if hurtful situations arise, everyone has agreed to meet and discuss what happened. If you do not have such an agreement, you can begin now, by asking the other(s) to join you for an exchange, knowing that the goals are understanding and forgiveness. When you and the other(s) involved are ready to talk, gather in a quiet place and sit across from one another, or in a circle.

1. Using "I" language, one person briefly explains how he feels injured or betrayed. Do not rehash the whole issue, blame the other, or become defensive, but state the particulars. "I feel hurt because you said I was a selfish person. It upsets me to think you believe that." Talk about how you feel.

2. The other person responds. He or she might say something like this, again using "I" language that focuses on the speaker's feelings. "I feel sad you don't spend more time with me. I miss doing things with you and sharing ideas like we used to."

3. Back and forth, the two communicate in a respectful way until understanding on both sides is reached.

4. If there are more than two people with grievances, the process is repeated until everyone has a chance to speak and receive a response.

5. Apologies are given. If it is felt, forgiveness is offered from each to the other(s). *An important part of forgiveness is the agreement that the matter will not be spoken of again.*

6. Take the other person's hands so that your palms are touching. Look each other in the eye for a moment.

7. Both people close their eyes and envision light coming from the source or the universe into their heart. It forms a spinning bubble of light that opens your heart even more to unconditional love.

8. Feel the energy of love flowing from your heart, down your arms, into your partner's hands. Keep all your attention on the feeling of love and the flow of energy into your partner. If your attention wanders, bring it gently back.

9. Know that you are giving and receiving energy and love at the same time, without needing to know how that happens. Essentially, you become one vibrating experience of unconditional love. Enjoy the exchange of this flow for as long as you wish.

10. When one partner feels complete, he slowly withdraws his hands. The other person does the same.

11. The two partners look each other in the eye again, and then embrace. Share your experience. Take a few

minutes to tell your partner the highlights of what you felt or realized. Then receive what your partner shares with you.

12. Repeat the whole process with each person involved.

Community healing and forgiveness

I once had the privilege of observing a traditional Huna rite called Ho'oponopono, conducted by a native Hawaiian healer. The purpose of the ceremony was to make right relationships where there was disharmony, and forgiveness was a central part of the healing ritual. There were many families in that room, each waiting for a ceremony with the healer. Everyone watched while each group went through the steps. If a family member was ill, angry, or unhappy, he or she would explain the circumstances to all.

The healer would ask other family members or friends their view of the cause of the imbalance. Illness, distress, and interpersonal problems were seen as a community problem. Healing could not take place only with the individual. Practical suggestions were given. Then, the healer would point out where forgiveness was needed, and lead each person in forgiving him- or herself and the others. Prayers and chants brought the family ancestors into the process. Healing energies were invoked, and gratitude was expressed. It was a thorough process that could take several hours per group, but everyone was patient, even the children. Traditional Ho'oponopono has been modified and incorporated into modern psychotherapy with good results.

You also may utilize the Forgiveness Exchange with your family, which is a Western modification of the Hawaiian ceremony. Gather together when you have plenty of time. Some families start with a general discussion of future family plans or schedules, or other "business" that includes the children's and parents' needs and wishes. After the practical aspects of the meeting are covered, one parent asks if anyone has felt out of balance with another family member. If so, they begin the exercise.

Embrace radical forgiveness

The act of forgiveness is mysterious. There are those who genuinely forgive the most heinous acts, while others cannot imagine how that could be possible. Forgiveness is the highest form of love. It is based on the principle that we all are vulnerable to making mistakes and we can identify with the person who has erred. To forgive ourselves we need to reach deep into our core and find the parts of ourselves that we can love. Psychologically speaking, to forgive someone, including yourself, is to be freed from an unhealthy emotional bond of resentment.

This form of love is possible even in the most horrible of situations. I heard of a man whose family member had been murdered. This is an experience I know well, as I lost my sister to a violent crime. The man, after being eaten up by anger for more than a decade over the murder of his family member, happened one day to be seated in first class on an airplane with the Dalai Lama. Knowing he needed to be freed from his anger, he sent a note on a napkin over to one of the Dalai Lama's assistants asking to speak to His Holiness, explaining the situation. The assistant motioned him over, and he explained his inability to forgive to the Dalai Lama, who nodded and said he understood this feeling very well—that in China's occupation of Tibet, many people he loved had been murdered. What I do, he said, is to picture them as children, and then I cannot be angry. This means that even if someone becomes truly "evil," at one point, it was not so. To forgive them at any point of their existence is still forgiveness.

When we found out that a family friend and business associate had murdered my sister, Judy, I was in shock. Her daughter and her husband were enraged, but I felt nothing because I was numb. When I finally could feel something, it wasn't anger, but an overwhelming sadness and desolation.

When you lose someone you love through violence, the world no longer seems a safe place. I still cannot watch movies or news programs with even the slightest mention of violence. For many months, I worked to find any kind of feeling for my sister's murderer, and found only bland neutrality.

One day during the lengthy trial of my sister's murderer, he stood up from the prisoner's table in the courtroom as the guard directed him to leave. I happened to stand at the same time. Ten feet apart, we faced each other. Eye-to-eye, without facial expression from either of us, it seemed as if we were communicating soul-to-soul. There was no message, no sense of the other as a personal self—it was simply one soul recognizing another. That moment brought the first feeling I had for him and what he had done—compassion. It has been six years now, and on the few occasions I think of this man, it is with compassion in my heart.

If you are in a situation that requires radical forgiveness, try the following exercise.

Exercise: Forgive from a Distance

It is possible to unburden oneself from the shackles of re-sentment you may feel toward someone you will never con-tact again or who has passed away. Neither time nor distance limits the self-healing benefits of forgiveness, so it's never too late to do this for yourself. Also consider that the person you are addressing may receive your statement of forgiveness energetically.

1. Find a quiet place. Have your journal and a pen ready.

2. Imagine that the person you are forgiving is sitting in front of you now. Notice all the details of her face and the way she is sitting. Use your memory to make it real.

3. Write in your journal what you would like to say to this person. Write as you would speak, naturally and openly. Be truthful. Write what you feel.

4. Start by describing your feelings of resentment or an-ger, and how it's affected your life. Then describe how you've tried to work through these feelings.

5. When you come to a place where there are no more words, pause, and again envision this person sitting in front of you, with all the details.

6. Continue writing for as long as you need.

7. At some point you will know it's time to welcome your feelings of forgiveness, even if you have only a slight inclination to forgive. Write down how you came to this place, and what it feels like. Write everything you want to say.

8. End your writing with this statement: "I, [your name], forgive you, [his or her name]. I release us both into a new beginning."

9. Complete your session with a moment of silence. You may want to bless the person and yourself with unconditional love.

Make amends

Making amends is different from asking for forgiveness. The purpose of making sincere amends to someone you've harmed is to correct the harm you have done. Another benefit is that the person making amends is freed from guilt over past deeds. It's a process that is central to twelve-step programs such as Alcoholics Anonymous. The ninth step to recovery in the program says, "Made direct amends to such people whenever possible, except when to do so would injure them or others." For most, it's a profound experience. After self-reflection and preparation, a time is arranged to meet and the person making amends a) apologizes for each specific incident in detail, b) asks if there is anything he or she can do to remedy the harm, and c) asks if there is anything else the other person wants to discuss.

It doesn't matter if the recipient of the apology offers forgiveness or not, or if that person doesn't accept the apology completely—the one making amends has taken action to correct harmful behavior. Taking this action also implies that you have learned from your mistakes and will be mindful not to repeat them.

Don wanted to make amends, so he made another phone call to his wife and daughter, this time asking for their forgiveness for the way he had treated them. He told them he didn't want to have dialysis and that he was dying. There was no response, and he was even more depressed during our visit.

At seven the next morning, my cell phone rang. It was Dorothy, his helper, who told me that Don had died during the night. She found him in his bed. An empty bottle of pain pills was on the bed stand.

I wondered what had been going through Don's mind when he took his own life. I hoped his passage had been easy and that as he died he experienced the religious imagery he connected so deeply with. Perhaps the promise of a new life in heaven with Christ was more attractive to him than struggling with the decision about dialysis. Sometimes people fear pain and dissolution toward the end of the dying process. And it could be that his wife's inability to forgive him, or his inability to forgive himself, was too heavy to bear. In any case, he had made his choice—to be fully in charge of his own death.

He could not forgive himself before he was forgiven. Some might see his suicide as a failure to transform, and others might believe it was a good choice. Either way, his story illustrates the power of the presence and absence of forgiveness.

Although your need or yearning for forgiveness may not be as strong as Don's, take the time to decide where it is called for in your life. As you continue to work with forgiveness, you are walking yourself out of the dark forest and toward a place of peace and wholeness.

CHAPTER 9

Use Your Imagination

When you start preparing for death you soon realize that you must look into your life now . . . and come to face the truth of yourself. Death is like a mirror in which the true meaning of life is reflected.

—Sogyal Rinpoche, *The Tibetan Book of Living and Dying*

Imagery and active imagination are incredibly powerful tools for inner work. When we surrender to the flow of our creative intelligence and trust that it will guide us to healing and transformation, we are able to let go and witness an outpouring of meaningful images that we can interact with. This process can uncover truths about ourselves that might otherwise go undiscovered. And once we trust the flow of images from our unconscious to our conscious mind, or from the collective unconscious—the memory of humankind—to our personal unconscious, the practice of imagery becomes a valued guide we can depend upon. Yet, this process of working with imagery appears to be so simple, I sometimes have difficulty convincing clients to try it.

I believe that imagery is our primary means of sensing and

experiencing the world. If you look around the space you're in you will notice that except for organic matter, every object in your view once was an image in someone's mind, before they made it into a chair, an arch in the doorway, a pattern in the rug—and the rug itself. Before the use of written and spoken language, our ancestors used gestures to communicate, which in themselves are images. They also left iconic artwork on cave walls and rocks, on jewelry, tools, and pots, images that communicate their lives to us thousands of years later.

We are primed to learn and communicate with others and ourselves through images as much as we are endowed with capabilities of language and thought. "One picture is worth a thousand words." A child begins learning through picture books that contain messages and stories.

Active imagination and imagery have played a role in the work I've done with all of the clients whose stories are in this book, so by reading their stories, you have already gained a sense of how this practice works. Here are a few guidelines you will find helpful in working with the exercises in this chapter.

1. Focus on and listen to your images; they have a life of their own and are very real. They will reveal themselves to you when you listen.
2. Stick with one image long enough to have a full experience, even though other images may attract you.
3. Don't prematurely interpret what comes. Work with the raw data just as it is. Notice and then record what happens.
4. Don't censor or hold back anything, no matter how foreign or difficult the imagery and feelings. Trust. Enjoy the amazing creativity that flows through you.

What is imagination?

The imagination is the meeting place between our unconscious and conscious minds. Deep within us are unknown emotions, images, and thought patterns that are sequestered away and therefore unconscious. In active imagination and imagery work, we invite this material to come forward into the space of the imagination so we can work with it consciously.

Working within the imaginal realm began with the shamans of ancient times and is still practiced by shamans in nontechnological societies throughout the world. They connect to deities and natural forces to effect healings, crop growth, and successful hunts through their imagination. Some have an imaginative power so strong that they create the experience of shape-shifting into a bird or animal that travels to other places to retrieve remedies or information for healing. The shamans help people heal and transform by interacting with a person's inner world. What we call "imagination" they call a "state of being," or a literal place where communication with other realms can occur. What happens in imaginative encounters is very real, and has real effects in the real world. These encounters inspire rituals and ceremonies, and often direct the community ethics.

Active imagination, a practice in which a person interacts with images from the unconscious, was central to the early Islam religion and now is practiced mainly by the mystical sect of Sufism. The poet Coleridge, Jakob Böhme, and Swedenborg, among other Western philosophers and teachers, championed the value of the imaginative realm.

In the 1900s Carl Jung developed active imagination as a technique of psychotherapy, with the goal of making unconscious elements available to the conscious mind, as well as communicating between the personal and collective unconscious. He applied it through dreamwork, visualizations, automatic writing, and art. Another modern scholar who enriched the body of knowledge about the imagination was Henri Corbin.

Each of these original thinkers promoted specific ideas about what constituted active imagination. Here I am using the terms *active imagination*, *imagery*, and *visualization* interchangeably to describe any focused inner process that engages the imagination. But one word I want to be sure to avoid conflating with this concept is *fantasy*. We all know what fantasy is—random images of and daydreaming about events that we notice and feel. There is no intervention in fantasy; we are carried along in the stream of what comes into our minds.

In active imagination, we select an image, feeling, or thought and begin to focus and work with it. When you used Voice Dialogue to interact with your selves, you were doing a form of active imagination. Imagery is at the core of energy medicine. Our purpose is to let the images and thoughts and feelings unfold so we can experience them as profoundly as possible. This practice has the power to transform us mentally, physically, and spiritually.

Exercise: Create Your Sanctuary

This exercise will open your imagination. As simple as it is, it will reveal feelings and ideas that may surprise you. Again, the key is to let go and honor whatever presents itself in your awareness, without censoring. Have fun!

1. Have your journal and pen nearby. Sit or lie down in a quiet place where you won't be disturbed. You may play meditative music if you wish.

2. Close your eyes and take seven deep breaths, relaxing your jaw, shoulders, and belly. Let out each breath as slowly as you can. Then breathe normally.

3. Invite images of a special room you are creating just for yourself. It can be any kind of room at all. Give up any ideas of what a room should have in it and just notice what comes.

4. Notice the external structure. Are there walls or windows, or does something else form the structure? Use any material you wish.

5. Look around the room. Is it sparsely furnished, or ornate? How does it feel overall? Does it remind you of anything? Look at specific objects, noticing colors, textures, and materials.

6. Consciously open all your senses—hearing, sight, touch, smell, and taste—in your room. This practice helps you to notice the subtleties of your environment and your mind.

7. In your mind's eye, walk around and touch things in your environment, remembering how they feel and how you feel about them.

8. Find a place to be comfortable and quiet in your room. Be there for a while.

9. Know that you can come back to your sanctuary at any time. You can come here to rest, meditate, create, or problem-solve.

10. Write about and draw your experience in your journal. With practice, you will learn to trust your imagination and the wisdom that comes from entering a quiet state of being. You may be surprised at how easily creativity and solutions to problems arise from this place of sanctuary. Above all, you will develop a portable place of peacefulness.

Jennifer, a forty-four-year-old client of mine, had good results from doing the preceding exercise. She was a psychiatrist on the academic staff in the department of child and adolescent psychiatry at a university, and was known for her interest in alternative medicine and psychotherapies. Her graduate students appreciated her quick humor and creative teaching style.

She had metastatic breast cancer that had spread to her liver. She was symptom-free, but being a physician, she knew that soon she would begin to feel the effects of the cancer. Over a period of four years she had received five types of chemotherapy; the lesions would shrink or disappear after one chemo agent, then reappear and multiply. The ambiguity of being told the tumors had shrunk and then later being told they had grown again was difficult for her, as it is for everyone who waits anxiously for treatment results.

When Jennifer created her special room, she was horrified to discover behind a bloodred door a dark room filled with trash. In a corner under a pile of old clothes she discovered a live fetus with a withered umbilical cord. "Oh, no!" she suddenly said. "This is my baby!" She bolted into a sitting position and opened her eyes. "It's my baby. I had it and put it in the room and forgot about it!" she exclaimed. "I forgot my baby." She was surprised at her strong emotional response to the image.

She explained that she had practiced Zen and Tibetan meditation for many years, and felt that she had "trained out" strong emotional feelings in favor of equanimity. And her analytical mind, which had dominated her years of medical school, caused her to ignore her feelings in favor of reason. This forgotten fetus, she interpreted, represented deep feminine feeling and being—Eros.

"My logos—logic—killed off my natural feminine energy," she said. "And my inner child has been neglected and abandoned."

When I asked her to tell me more about the room she had constructed and the fetus she had discovered in her vision, she began to cry. "It's all so meaningful," she said, "and I'm very moved, but not sure why. I can interpret the fetus as finding the vulnerable, undeveloped part of myself that needs nurturing. But that's not why I'm crying. It feels like an ocean of tears."

"Sometimes we cry when we come home to ourselves. You don't need to figure out the particulars now; just open to your feelings," I responded.

I gave Jennifer oil pastels and paper, and invited her to draw what wanted to come forward regarding her vision. She was pleased with her art, showing me a swirl of multicolored swatches around the edges of the paper, with a sun on one side and a moon on the other; in the center was a female figure holding a baby swaddled in a bright red blanket.

"The red blanket means life," she said. "And the baby has already grown from a fetus. And the mother—me—is taking care of it. Sure feels good."

Jennifer continued to go back to the sanctuary she had

created, and each time, it changed. Gone was the trash. The red door changed to a blue one that opened into a seaside grotto. She used her special room as a reliable starting place to discover what and who from her unconscious wanted to come forward to interact with her.

Be open to the surprises you may encounter in your personal sanctuary, and know that whatever comes forward is a truth that invites your exploration. Sometimes the images come so quickly that we dismiss them as unimportant. On the contrary, a quick flash of an image can be just as productive to explore as one that stays longer in our awareness. Inner work, especially imagery, proceeds more quickly than the passage of time in our "outer" life.

Making changes through imagination

Another person I worked with was Thomas, who had been ill since childhood. He had a negative outlook on life, believing that he never would be happy, have a girlfriend or a good job, or become well. Nothing seemed positive to him. At our first meeting he told me he was "hopeless." He had tried various therapies and said he knew I couldn't help him either. He felt bombarded by images of impending disaster—a terrorist attack, a burglar coming through his bedroom window at night, an auto accident, or worst of all, images of his body deteriorating into death. I felt compassion for him because he could not experience even a glimmer of hope about anything. His psychiatrist had prescribed several medications, but none eliminated his symptoms entirely.

I told him that since he was so good at creating imagery, it was worthwhile to try to introduce a few positive and helpful visualizations. He was resistant at first, but after much work, he was able to have meaningful interactions with others and himself in the imaginal realm. The inner sanctuary he created was a psychedelic painted room where he played drums to loud hip-hop music. He said that visualizing being there and playing his music reduced his anxiety and gave him a tiny bit of hope that someday he might have a normal life.

Using imagery with children to create behavioral changes is very effective because they are in touch with their imagination and it's fun for them. Many years ago when I was a probation officer for young gang members, I used active imagination to help them change their self-image. Immersed in an environment of fractured families, crime, and a probable future of welfare subsistence, they could not conceive of a life beyond the ghetto. Through imagery we worked on social skills, job training, and a vision of themselves succeeding in school and as adults. At first the practice felt foreign and useless to them, but after a while they would ask for it in our sessions.

One girl, Altagracia, practiced a visualization of herself studying math and then holding her report card and seeing a B grade. At the end of the semester, she surprised herself by raising her grade from a D to an A. She said imagining herself studying and getting a good grade helped her to settle down and learn the material. "The imagery made me want to study," she reported. "I finally believed I was smart enough to learn the stuff."

Another young person on my caseload was DeShaun, age sixteen, who was in a gang that his father and three older brothers belonged to. He had seen all four go to jail repeatedly for drug trafficking and burglary. But he had never been caught

when he participated in illegal gang activities. He was on probation for truancy. He told me that his dream was to "get out of
the neighborhood and get a real job downtown in an office." In
his imagery, he practiced seeing and feeling himself dressed
nicely and working as a clerk at the Los Angeles City Hall. Low
self-esteem had kept him from applying to the summer mentor-
ship work programs for youth. After a month of practice, he
had enough confidence to apply for a position. He was immediately accepted, and began working part-time as a clerk trainee
in a building across from city hall.

Exercise: Rehearsal Imagery

*In rehearsal imagery, you use your imagination to rehearse
a skill, learning to perform it better through inner practice.
When you watch the Olympics you will often see a com-
petitor close his eyes before entering the arena, mentally
doing his moves perfectly. I know a solo violinist who "practices" ten minutes twice a day while lying down on her
couch. She hears the music of the concerto and inwardly
sees her fingers moving on the fingerboard to match the
notes. She says that when she next practices with her violin
her skills have improved.*

Chess players often rehearse advanced moves and
sequences inwardly, seeing and anticipating probable
moves of their inner opponent. Since the game of chess is
timed, rehearsal helps players recognize opportunities
for sophisticated plays more quickly. I even taught imagery to an oil field worker who needed to practice the

steps of capping a gusher without seeing the pipe fittings, because his goggles would be covered with oil. When we use our imagination in rehearsal, our brains, nerves, muscles, and minds respond as if we were actually performing the activity. Here are the steps for rehearsing a skill with imagery.

1. Get into a relaxed position in a quiet place.

2. Close your eyes. Pick a skill or interaction you want to rehearse. It can be anything, such as:

   - a difficult conversation with a partner or your family

   - participating in a social event without tiring

   - graduating from using a wheelchair to a cane

   - arising early—energized and ready to meet the day

   - easily completing a treatment of dialysis or chemo

3. Create a scene and place yourself and all the elements of the event in it. You are in your body, doing the activity.

4. Initiate the conversation or activity in your mind's eye. Open all your senses.

5. See, feel, and hear yourself *successfully* doing the activity.

6. Continue the rehearsal until it feels natural to stop. If you come to a place where you get stuck, stop and start over.

7. Repeat the activity or a portion of the activity until you feel complete. Several short rehearsals throughout the day are better than one long one.

8. At the end of the rehearsal see yourself feeling happy and satisfied with your success. Congratulate yourself!

9. Bring the rehearsal into action in your life when you feel ready. You may repeat or modify the rehearsal as often as you wish.

Imagery even has played an influential part in the world of science. There are examples of scientists who have received images in dreams that were central to important discoveries. It is said that Friedrich Kekule saw a three-dimensional model of the molecular structure of benzene in a dream, and that during a nap Einstein saw the image of the formula $E = mc^2$ written in the air. I have done brainstorming sessions with corporate management, screenwriters, and others using the techniques of imagery and visualization.

When we are ill and aware of our mortality, we are presented with many physical and interpersonal problems. We can utilize our imagination to come up with solutions that would not occur to us through logic alone.

The following exercise can be used to explore the nature of any challenge or problem, and if you give yourself wholeheartedly to it, accepting the images, feelings, and thoughts that come, your creative intelligence will respond even more fully. With practice and trust, you'll soon be able to enjoy the fruits of your imagination.

Exercise: Problem Solving with Imagery

1. Find a quiet place. Have your journal, a pen, and oil pastels or felt-tip pens nearby. Play quiet ambient music at a low volume for the entire exercise.

2. Sit or lie down in a comfortable position. Close your eyes. Relax your jaw, shoulders, and belly.

3. Take seven slow, deep breaths and release any tension in your body.

4. Silently ask your inner wisdom to present you with a *single image that represents your problem.* Your statement should be simple and specific, such as, "I'm ready to receive an image that symbolizes my failing marriage," or, "Show me an image that represents how I feel about being trapped in this bed."

5. As you relax even more, images will begin to enter your mind. Be patient until the flow of images comes. Place all your attention on the first one that comes. Hold it in your attention as long as you can, even if it changes. If thoughts enter or other images appear, bring your attention back to the original image. Stay with it long enough to notice color, texture, details, and the feelings you relate to it. Don't worry if the image doesn't make sense to you; just stick with it.

6. Open your eyes and record everything you remember under the heading "Problem." You may draw simple diagrams or use colored pens, as well as write descriptions of what appears. Then write words or phrases of any associations you have to the image. Take your time.

7. Close your eyes again and take four or five deep breaths, relaxing even more. Ask your inner wisdom to present you with an image that represents *what you are meant to learn* from this problem. Open your mind to whatever comes, without expectation. Hold this second image in your mind to notice everything about it, including your feelings.

8. Open your eyes and record the results with a drawing of the image and phrases about it under the heading "Lesson." Include all the details and your feelings as you work with it.

9. Close your eyes again and take four or five deep breaths, relaxing even more. Ask your inner wisdom to present you with an image that brings you closer to the solution of this problem. Accept the image without censoring or changing it.

10. Open your eyes and draw the image under the heading "Solution." Write down your associations and feelings about the image.

11. Breathe deeply again. Then continue writing whatever comes to your mind regarding the solution of your problem. Stay open and receive all information, even if it is contradictory or doesn't make sense. You already have produced valuable material; see what more wants to come that relates to the solution. You may pause and go inward and request another image if it's needed.

12. End with a feeling of gratitude for your inner wisdom. Completing this exercise has already changed the problem. You have created a cooperative relationship with the problem and have received more information about it. Because you are more familiar with the issues involved, you probably will be less fearful of them. You may have developed more helpful attitudes about the challenge and become aware of limiting ideas and feelings. You may repeat any part of the exercise at another time to continue working toward a satisfactory solution if needed.

Creative imagination

All work with the imagination is creative. The imagination is used to create works of art and literature, but in some the process of imagination shows up as a central part of the plot or art piece itself. In *Alice's Adventures in Wonderland*, a young girl falls down a rabbit hole into a world where creatures and events appear and behave in ways that are incomprehensible to the "real" world. We can say that she encounters her unconscious, which operates with supreme freedom and easily generates material for her to interact with. Alice rises to the occasion with each encounter, dealing with her sense of awe, fear, and happiness in a world that makes no sense. In *The Fall of the House of Usher*, Edgar Allan Poe creates a gothic tale filled with inexplicable, illogical events that are startling.

The surrealist paintings of Salvador Dalí are another portrayal of the inexhaustible magnitude of creative imagery that exists below the level of our conscious mind. His provocative images are associated with feelings and thoughts that also are unconscious.

A client of mine said, "Before I die, I want to know what else is in there—what is me that I don't know about." In the last months of his life, he created drawings and clay sculptures, poetry, and short stories based on the images he encountered. He said he was surprised how much he enjoyed creating from the rich material he discovered in his unconscious. At his memorial, his family displayed his art and read from his written works, making his memorial a unique life celebration.

Remember, this is your time to explore your creativity and the undiscovered parts of yourself. Even though you are ill, you have a natural drive within to grow and transform and discover. When your time is short, you quickly let go of "the small stuff" and focus on what's important. Along with exchanging love with your family and friends and getting your affairs in order, doing your inner work is the most important way you can spend your days. Most people at the end of life find that without the barriers of ego and everyday distractions, they can easily tap into creative imagination.

You already have used focused imagination in some of the previous exercises that have specific purposes, such as bringing in healing energies and guided meditation. Now we'll move into more open practices that will help us peek into that rabbit hole to see what's happening, and ask our inner wisdom to bring up images that will be meaningful for our growth.

Exercise: Petition an Image for Growth

1. Sit or lie down in a comfortable position. If you want to have ambient music, turn on the player. Have your journal and pen nearby.

2. Close your eyes. Take seven deep breaths, letting each out as slowly as you can. It usually takes that long for the calmer parasympathetic nervous system to take over from the more activating sympathetic system. Deep breathing does it! Then breathe normally. Let go of tension in your shoulders, jaw, and belly. Relax all your muscles.

3. Say to yourself something like, "I invite my inner wisdom to present me with an image that's appropriate for my growth."

4. Notice what comes. If several images come, pick the one that attracts you the most. It could be a person, an object, an animal, or an abstract design. One may be more interesting or frightening or just stand out more than the others. Sometimes only one image comes. Don't censor an image because it seems unimportant or weird. You also may open the door to your sanctuary and go inside to engage what's there.

5. Hold the one image in your awareness, noticing everything about it.

6. Write down your feelings and associations about the image.

7. Ask the image what it has to teach you, what it wants you to know.

8. Listen! Take in the information even though it might not make sense yet.

9. Prompt the image for more information by asking it questions, like number 7.

10. If it feels too dangerous to engage a particular image, let it go and pick another. Trust your intuition. Write down what didn't feel right—that's valuable material also.

11. When you are finished, write down everything you remember in your journal to ground the experience. Make drawings.

12. Decide how to bring some part of the experience into your daily life. If I receive an image of an elephant, I might tell a friend about it, or study about the habits of elephants, or place a photo of elephants on my refrigerator door so the image saturates my awareness every time I walk by. I could go to the zoo and observe

elephants, or make up a children's story about a baby elephant, which might reveal deeper psychological material. I could put on some meditative music and take on elephantine energies and movement in dance. Bringing an image into action opens us to unknown possibilities. It's creative expression in service of learning about ourselves.

Active imagination

In our movement toward wholeness, other psychological functions can become enhanced. For instance, another benefit of doing active imagination in an open, creative way is that it develops our intuition. We become skilled at making a space for images, ideas, and insights to arise spontaneously, which is the mechanism of all intuitive process. We are open to the flow of our inner life and the collective consciousness, so at the right moment a meaningful image or thought catches our attention.

A client of mine who became very skilled at active imagination, Jennifer, was ready to explore her feelings about death. Her Buddhist training had taught her death was not to be feared because although the body and the conscious mind die, the deeper subtle mind continues existence and is reborn into a new person. But her psychiatric training suggested she might have other strong feelings about death that were unconscious. She said she did not fear dying, but like most of us, did not want to suffer in the process. She wanted to find out if she had suppressed any fears about dying.

"Tell yourself that you welcome images, feelings, and thoughts about your own death," I said. "Lie down, let the couch support you, and begin the deep breathing I taught you. Tell yourself that you're ready to receive information that will be helpful for your growth."

She chose to have the experience without music, to try visualization without stimulus. Her breathing started with deep inhalations and exhalations, then calmed to shallow, regular movements of her chest. By her rapid eyelid movements back and forth, I knew she was seeing imagery.

"I have a fire stick in my hand. It's very hot. Have to hang on to the torch," she whispered. "I'm climbing over black boulders, looking for something—a cave, I think. It's cold and I'm a little afraid. There are night noises and the air is damp. I'm wearing sandals, so . . . I don't want to slip." After an interval of silence, she continued reporting.

"Yes, an opening under the boulder . . . going in . . . Oh—it stinks . . . like dead animals and mold." I prompted her to look around, and reminded her that she could leave at any time.

"Bones . . . and human skulls . . . and an altar or something like that. Rolls of paper with symbols on them . . . Oh—my torch—the flame is getting small."

Her experience continued as she systematically searched through the cave. She objectively examined the human skulls and animal bones, and icons of worship she found on the altar. The symbols on the scrolls fascinated her, but evoked strong anxiety. Throughout it all, she felt hypervigilant, but not fearful until the torch flame extinguished. At that moment, she panicked and stumbled up the rocky path to the entrance. When she came out of the cave, felt the sunshine, and breathed clean air, she was relieved. She opened her eyes slowly and looked around. "I'm really happy to be here with you," she said. "The vision was very real."

One by one, we reviewed her feelings about what she had encountered. We talked about how the torch symbolized the flame of consciousness bringing her into the cave. I shared the Australian myth of Sun Woman, who carries her torch from the east each morning toward the west, lighting the sky in an arc, and then she goes underground and carries it back toward the east. The chthonic, underground journey is important, for she gives energy to the plants and underground creatures every day so they can grow. Her work with the cycles of light and dark, above- and belowground, brings balance to the earth.

In her vision, Jennifer experienced the darkness as a velvety cloak that engulfed her in warmth and protection; the skulls and bones didn't evoke emotion, probably because in medical school she worked with cadavers, she said. It was the paper scrolls and ritual objects that brought deep feelings of awe and anxiety, which then transformed into fear. "If I knew what was written on them, I wouldn't be so afraid," she said. "I don't like not knowing."

"Perhaps that's your fear of death," I offered. "Your fear of the unknown."

I suggested that at home she put herself into a relaxed state, which she knew how to do, and recall the image of the scrolls. Asking her inner wisdom to show her truth, she could read the essential message inscribed on the paper. If and when the words began to flow, she should act as a scribe, recording what came. The language could be simple or even just partial phrases—or images. Without censoring, she could record what came into her mind, whatever it might be.

At her next session, I was touched by Jennifer's connection to the translation she had made from the scroll. She felt that the message she had read in the scrolls predicted her imminent death. She was sad to think of her demise as a reality that might happen soon, because she hoped she would live for several years. The intensity of the scroll message for her, which invited her to accept death, put her in a vulnerable state. After a few tears, she was quiet.

Earlier, before our session, I also had entered her vision to translate the scrolls. I heard the crackling of the ancient paper. I focused on the faded calligraphy and strange symbols, holding them in my awareness. The words came quickly. I shared my translation with her:

> Expect to be surprised in your earthly incarnation, for the laws of stone and vegetation, of moving waters, thermal tides from the sun, and all dense matter comprising material worlds such as yours are capricious. Not because of a careless or uncaring God, but for your soul's development. Without serendipity there is no creativity. Without darkness, there is no light. Without death, there is no life. Both life and death are part of the same continuum.
>
> Your consciousness seeks contrast, and that necessitates chaos. Meeting this constant flux and flow of unpredictable energies with grace and passion is soul work. It is your work. Make your heart and mind as open as the cloudless sky and trust. Make this open transparency your center. Hold nothing back. Know that all ways to the end are equal; it's the quality of your journey through this incarnation that is weighed on the great scale of justice—measured, praised, and

redeemed after death by you, from the depth of your
compassionate wisdom.

Out of all the permutations and combinations of messages
we could have read from the scrolls, we each created a piece that
had meaning, that came from the depths of our being initiated
by imagery. Individually, we chose a phrase from our writing to
meditate on. I picked "All ways to the end are equal; it's the
quality of your journey . . ."

"Yes, I understand. Enlightenment can come in many ways,"
Jennifer said. "And I can be myself—all of who I am. What a
relief!"

We came out of the meditation at the same time, and she
said, "I'm not running from death anymore. It's real. It could
happen tomorrow or next month, and it's time I accept it." I
told her that we should prepare for both life and death. Hugging
her, I congratulated her on her good work.

When I saw her a month later, she was in bed at home. The
cancer was taking its toll, and another round of chemotherapy
had weakened her. She had lost patches of hair. Plastic bags of
nourishment, pain medication, and saline solution hung from
the chrome IV tree. Her students were taking shifts to care for
her, and as the helper of the day left the bedroom, Jennifer told
me that all the campus religious clubs were praying for her recovery. "It's funny," she commented, "that they don't think of
praying for my easy death. Some days I say my Buddhist prayers
and I'm quite ready to go, but other times I get hooked on everything I'll miss when I'm gone."

"What will you miss?"

"My students' faces. Their eagerness. My patients. My Buddhist teachers. The sound of the Tibetan meditation gong. Walking meditation in the Zen garden. Everything in nature. Laughing with friends. Oh . . . so much I'll miss."

Jennifer's speech was becoming slurred, but she said she wanted to talk. She was concerned about her two spiritual teachers; each had offered to help her through the dying process with traditional rituals and prayers, and neither knew she also was studying with the other. In fact, they had no idea of her dedication to both Zen and Tibetan Buddhism. She told me she would like to have guidance and blessings from both, and to have the two of them present at the moment of her death. She suspected the Tibetan death rituals involved complex chants, and reading of passages from *The Tibetan Book of the Dead*, as well as sound from gongs and horns, all designed to help her consciousness leave her body and enter a realm that would ensure a good rebirth. The Zen tradition doesn't teach reincarnation, she explained. This teacher would probably encourage her to attain a deep state of meditation, which would exist as essential consciousness, even when her body and mind died.

She said that her Tibetan Buddhist teacher was scheduled for a visit that morning to give her initial instruction in Phowa. "It's a special practice used while dying so that our essential consciousness exits the body and gross mind in a state of peace," she said.

I asked her to tell me more about it.

"I've read just a little about it. I think my geshe [teacher] leads me in a visualization of the Buddha, with light coming from him into me. I'm supposed to feel Buddha's presence and connect with him. Then my teacher reads special texts from *The Tibetan Book of the Dead* that purify me from negative karma, grant me forgiveness, help me die a peaceful death, and through my death bring benefit to all beings everywhere. I'm sure I've oversimplified the practice, but I expect it'll be very powerful. And there's another one—the guru meditation—that he'll lead me through."

"I can tell this is important for you."

"Yes, really important. The state of mind we have at death decides which realm we're reborn into—which we've talked about. It's interesting because that's the same goal my Zen teacher talks about—a peaceful death."

When I returned, the nurse informed me that Jennifer had been in a coma for two days. I was happy that she'd had her visit with her Tibetan teacher. Apparently, a few hours after he left, she went into the coma. Her students were there grieving, knowing that the end was near. Her Tibetan teacher and Zen master were on the way.

I sat next to Jennifer's bed, put my hand on her heart, and gave her the energy of unconditional love. A few days earlier I had told her how much I valued our relationship and time together; I had thanked her for her trust in me, and for sharing the depth of who she was. At that time, she said she loved me as the dearest of friends and thanked me for helping her discover things about herself that were meaningful. We had shared tears and good-byes. And now, it was time for her to make the passage, that mysterious journey that beckons to each of us from the day we are born.

Meditating, I reached a quietude that felt like gentle undulations caressing the bottom of the sea. It was a wonderful state that lasted about half an hour. Her uneven breathing pulled me back into the room. The nurse was on the other side of the bed.

I matched my breathing to my friend's, keeping a still mind and heart, and joined her in her last exhalation.

I hope reading this chapter will enable you to use your imagination freely while doing the exercises. Not only will you learn new things about yourself that may have been hidden; you also will experience a delightful sense of play. Imagination is a healing art that reveals deep truths and augments our search for wholeness.

CHAPTER 10

Entering Dreamtime

Watching a peaceful death of a human being re-
minds us of a falling star; one of a million lights in
a vast sky that flares up for a brief moment, only
to disappear into the endless night forever.

—Elisabeth Kübler-Ross, *On Death and Dying*

When our psyche is presented with the news that we have a
limited time to live, the veil between our unconscious
and conscious minds becomes thinner, and the dream world
becomes more accessible. This is a rich time of exploring our
dreams; it's as if our wisdom wants to flood us with images
and information to accelerate our growth. There is a natural
withdrawal from the outer world into the inner reaches of
the imaginal realm, of which dreams are a major part. Death
brings us this gift, the ability to enter what some indigenous people call "dreamtime" more easily. And these journeys
bring us truth and meaning about who we are and how we
have lived.

The practice of dreamwork is so rich and varied, and can
be viewed from so many philosophical and scientific stances,
it's impossible to cover the myriad techniques available for

discovering the creative power of dreams. There are even disputes about what a dream is. But we've all been fascinated by their magic and curious about what they mean. Some dreams are inspirational, showing us possibilities for growth and wholeness that are surprising. Others have disturbing imagery or dream events that propel us into serious investigations about what's happening in our lives. In any case, our dreams always tell us the truth about the forces operating within us, in our outer lives, and within the collective unconscious of all humanity.

I encourage you to have an open mind, to start writing down your dreams and enjoy the exploration. Don't worry about the "right way" to do dreamwork or feel you're not an expert. Get to know your dreams—make a relationship with them by doing these exercises. Through practice you can improve your dream skills and spark the transformation that's inherent in dreamwork.

What is a dream?

Dreams are moving images, feelings, and thoughts that enter our consciousness as we sleep and that are laden with meaning. (I once had a client seriously say she didn't dream—she just watched pictures when she slept!) A dream is a living entity, filled with vitality and significance that is waiting to be explored further in your imagination and your body. Much like a ball of soft clay, it can be stretched and massaged into many forms so you see, feel, and experience it from different angles. It contains information that can be carried into action in your outer life. It can be inspirational, motivating, terrifying, or mundane. Because we are all connected, it is not just a singular event, but is related to everything in the history of your life, in the lives of people you know and don't know, and in the memory of humankind—the collective unconscious. It is a precious gift that should be honored.

I have a psychologist friend who has recorded and worked with her dreams for more than sixty years. On her bedroom bookshelves are rows of her dream journals, neatly numbered by year, that she started writing as a teenager. Journals from her early years are handwritten, and the later ones contain computer printouts. Each dream has a title, and each journal has an index of those titles. Some of them are cross-indexed. I felt privileged when she told me I had a special listing along with other friends who appeared regularly in her dreams. It's fascinating to see the themes and symbols that repeat themselves or change over a period of time. Dreams can initiate transformation and growth, and they in turn reflect the growth you have made.

In our busy lives, it takes time and effort to record and work with our dreams, yet it is one of the quickest, most fascinating ways to check in with yourself to get the truth of what you're feeling and needing, or what is waiting to develop in your consciousness. In most nontechnological cultures, the inner life of dreams is still considered to be as important, if not more so, than one's outer life. There, when you dream of someone, it is imperative to share that dream with him or her before proceeding with daily activities, because a dream can be a message from the gods or spirits, for either the dreamer or the person who is dreamed about, or for the community. A sacred dream message should be honored and delivered to the person in the dream. This is important not only to the people involved, but to the balance of energies in the whole tribe.

There are many theories about how to do dreamwork. My approach discourages immediate symbolic interpretation, or trying to figure out what each thing in the dream means. To me, deciding that one's dream of a lake only means such-and-such, as detailed in dream symbol books, is limiting. Too often there is a rush to "check off" a dream interpretation, but wise dreamers come back to their dreams after a time to enter them again, knowing that the dream has more to convey. Conventional dream interpretation satisfies the intellectual part of us that wants to know exactly what something means *now*. I suggest you take your time and do it only after you have explored experiential dreamwork.

Dreams are complex entities, with many levels of meaning, so several differing interpretations can arise for the dreamer. All are valuable. Only the dreamer is qualified to decide what meaning is in the dream; others can give their opinions, but the dreamer claims her or his understanding and meaning of the dream.

Remembering dreams

You need to remember your dreams to work with them, so writing them down in a journal is essential. The act of writing prompts your memory to provide more details, and also strengthens the bridge between your unconscious and conscious minds. Here are a few suggestions to help you remember your dreams.

Exercise: How to Remember Your Dreams

1. Each night before you go to sleep, sit on the edge of the bed and tell yourself over and over that you are ready to remember a dream. Five or six repetitions should help your inner dreamer awaken. You might say something like, "I'm ready to receive and remember a dream that will teach me about my next step in personal growth." Make your intention strong. Have your journal on the nightstand. Then lie down to sleep.

2. When you awaken, try to keep your body as close to its original position as possible. Then reach out for your journal and pen. If you wait until after you go to the bathroom to write it, your dream may go down the toilet!

3. Start writing what you remember, whether it's phrases, images, thoughts, or feelings. You don't need to write a logical sequence or story—just write what comes into your mind. Write as fast as you can, using a kind of shorthand and drawings if you can.

4. Value everything, no matter how inconsequential it may seem. Write details! Even a single image can initiate deep inner work.

5. Thank your inner wisdom for the dream, and reaffirm that you're ready to receive more.

If you are on certain kinds of medication or if you don't sleep well enough to reach the deeper stages of sleep that generate dreams, remembering them can be difficult. Some find that taking vitamin B6 helps increase the vividness of dreams and enhances dream recall. And of course, you want to do everything you can to attain quality sleep. If you've tried everything and still don't have a dream to put in your journal, be easy on yourself. Working with your imagination and the other modalities in previous chapters will take you where you need to go on your path to self-actualization.

The following exercise is a comprehensive initial approach to working with your dream. Answer each question fully, and leave space in your journal after each section to go back and add more.

Exercise: Elements of a Dream

Once you have recorded last night's dream in your journal, find time to go through the following steps, writing down your responses to each element. When you have completed this initial work, you will be more connected to the dream and will know a lot about it. Then you may wish to learn other techniques to continue to deepen your understanding.

CONTEXT: What was happening in your life when you had this dream? Were any significant or emotional events occurring?

TITLE: What title would you give to this dream? Don't think about it; just pick the first thing that pops into your mind.

FEELINGS: What feelings did you have during the dream? When you wrote the dream later? And what feelings come as you work with the dream now?

CHARACTERS: Who are the major players in the dream? Get to know them well, with as many details as possible. Whom in life do they remind you of? What parts of yourself do they represent?

ASSOCIATION: Some people, events, or objects in your dream may remind you of similar things in your life. Fully compare and explore these dream and "real"-life happenings and the meaning they hold for you.

THEME: What is the story line of your dream? Does this theme show up in your life these days? What did you learn about yourself? Explore the message of the dream.

ACTION: Is there any action to be taken or change to make in your life as a result of what you learned from this dream? Learn to trust the wisdom that is given to you in your dreams.

Dreamwork is an adventure

One client of mine found deep meaning in working with his dreams. Sonny was a forty-three-year-old man in good health who aspired to be a published poet. He had a wife and two young children, and made a living by driving an office supply delivery truck. He loved his family. They had fun together and enjoyed church activities. For the past eight months he had been plagued by nightmares, which made him anxious. He'd had one recent dream four times, and was frightened by what he thought it meant. "It's just like a Hitchcock movie," he said.

I suggested he close his eyes and see the images if he could, while he described the dream.

"Okay." He sighed and closed his eyes. "There are flocks of birds—large black ones like crows or ravens. I know there are exactly one hundred of them flying up out of the mist that covers the ground. As they fly up, they are circling around and around in a spiral that gets bigger and bigger. I'm really scared, because I know when they get up past the mist into clear sky, they'll turn around and come down to get me. It seems to take forever, and I'm in agony. Finally, they turn, pull back their wings, and dive, and I start screaming—I know I'll be killed. They circle down faster and faster, and all one hundred land on me at the same time. The sound is awful—flapping and cawing. I'm completely covered up with black bodies and fluttering wings. I can feel the pinch of their talons as they settle themselves. If you look at where I stand, all you see is a flapping tower of black birds. I'm so afraid. It's hard to breathe, because there's a musky, damp smell. I'm frozen. Afraid to move. I pray and pray for God to save me." He opened his eyes and hunkered down in the chair, staring at his lap. He let out a deep breath.

"Whoa. That's quite a dream. No wonder you were afraid. How do you feel now, after sharing your dream?"

"I feel sick to my stomach, and afraid. I think it means I'm going to die." He tapped his upper abdomen with his forefinger.

I asked Sonny to focus on the physical sensation in his belly, to stick with the feeling and see what happened. After a minute, he reported that the sick feeling was diminished. When I asked him if there was anything else happening, he became upset.

"There's one of those birds in there—shiny black, and it's

flapping around and pecking at my insides. I want it out! It's in my body."

"Keep all your attention there and just notice," I replied. After a while, he said that the bird had shrunk and wasn't causing any discomfort, but that it was still there and could eat his insides anytime. Continuing to notice, he connected to each part of the dream and allowed himself to feel what was there. I reflected back to him what he was reporting. Because the dreamer is in an altered state, this process is slow and thorough, interspersed with moments of silence. When he finished, I directed him to bring his attention back to the room.

"Okay. So what does the dream mean?" he asked. "What's the interpretation?"

"I don't know what it means," I answered. "We'll discover what it means to you. It's too soon to think about interpretation, because if we go there initially, the energy and exploratory value of the dream is lost and we end up stuck in mental gymnastics. The nature of dream is not verbal; it's the language of image, movement, energies, and feeling. Let's take our time and have you relate to the dream directly as you just did. Then if you're interested in the intellectual and cultural interpretation of the symbols, we can go there too."

He acquiesced. "Okay. But I'm telling you now, I think that bird in my stomach means I have cancer and I'm going to die from it." He became distressed again, and grabbed for the Kleenex. I waited until he finished crying.

"I understand your fear. Try to stay open as we continue working with the dream. We'll revisit it next week. Keep writing down all your dreams, and see if you're moved to create a poem about the raven."

Types of dreams

Some would classify Sonny's dream as an animal dream, and others would call it a fear dream. Dreams have been classified into types or categories since the beginning of modern psychology. I suppose our need to nail down what a dream is stems from our desire to conquer the elusive and unpredictable qualities of the dream. From the simple designation of a dream as a "fear" dream to sophisticated categories such as "compensatory" or "consolamentum" dreams, we seek to somehow capture a dream by categorizing it. In truth, because they are multilevel creations, dreams can fit into many categories, depending on how you look at them.

One type of dream that is important to people who know they are in the final stage of life is the predictive dream. Everyone is interested in dreams that foretell what will happen in the future, but it's especially poignant when a dying person dreams of his or her own death.

I've found that most terminally ill people I've worked with who pay attention to their dreams eventually have a predictive death dream. It may address their fear, or give them hope for life after death, or even present the circumstances and details of their passing. It's a blessing, because it gives the dreamer time to prepare for the transition. This predictive dream may come as early as six months before the person passes away. Sometimes it comes as a metaphor—she dreams she is packing for a trip or crossing an ocean, or talking with relatives who have passed away. Or it comes more directly, as with my friend Brugh, who dreamed that the Dalai Lama told him he would die soon. A few months later, the dream announcement came true.

What makes it confusing is that we also can have death dreams that are metaphors for personal transformation—the old ways dying off so the new energies can enter. We never know whether the death dream is literal or not, but the more we work with it, the more likely we are to know. And we can ask ourselves to dream a clarifying dream.

The night before my sister was murdered, I dreamed of how it happened, with all the details that later proved to be correct. I was leading a seminar, and for teaching purposes, I illustrated my dream of the murder and cut out the drawings to pin on the wall, showing how we can enter the energy of the dream. My drawing of the murderer's face was recognizable as the actual murderer's face. But my psyche protected me from the horror, and I viewed and interpreted the dream as a message about myself—my masculine part killing off the feminine part during a period of overwork. It took me a while to get over the guilt of not seeing the other, literal interpretation and warning my sister. I often have dreams of my clients' deaths before they occur, and many women have predictive dreams about being pregnant. Our psyches can alert us to significant events. In order to be aware of this we need to engage with our dreams.

Engage your dream

A dream should be savored. As you write it down, feel the delight in the creative images and feelings that have been presented to you. Work with it yourself first before sharing it with anyone else. Think of your dream as a ball of clay, and pull it into various shapes, noticing what it reveals with its various expressions.

The more you value and attend to your dreams, the more they will give you. There are many ways to enter a dream; the following exercise is one of my favorites.

Exercise: Becoming the Dream Symbol

This practice is found in many psychological systems and therapies. You can do this as a written exercise in your journal. Some choose to speak their thoughts out loud and record what they say during this exercise with audio equipment, because they learn even more by listening to the tone and intensity of their voice afterward. Others may want to take it a step further by setting up a video camera to bring visual cues to the character or object they are portraying. On the surface this may seem like acting, but I guarantee that if you let go of self-consciousness and allow the words and actions to flow, you'll have some surprises that will be insightful.

If you are working with a dream partner, he or she can witness your process. A friend or family member who is interested in dreams makes an ideal dream partner. Neither person needs to be an expert in dreamwork—interested, curious partners who are eager to learn and are committed to the process can develop skill and find meaning in their dreams by practicing the exercises in this chapter. Later, you may want to join a dream group, where you may learn different ways of working with your and others' dreams.

1. Close your eyes. Pick a character or object in the dream that is the most salient for you—what catches

your attention first? Visualize the character or object as clearly as you can.

2. Imagine and feel yourself easily entering the body of the dream character or object.

3. From this position, begin to speak out loud or write as this character or object. Start with your eyes closed. Then introduce yourself by saying, "I am the _____ in [your name]'s dream."

4. Continue talking as that character. Let the words come without hesitation or concern.

5. Perhaps you want to move as that character or object; you can do so in your mind's eye or actually move your body. Notice how you feel.

6. When you feel finished, stop and open your eyes if they were closed. Look around you. Make sure you are grounded and fully present to your surroundings.

7. Write down any thoughts you have about the material that came forward.

8. If you made a recording of your session, you may review it now or later.

9. Repeat the process with other characters or objects in the dream. As you work with each element in this way, more material and insights arise about feelings, associations, and themes in your life. The more you know about yourself and appreciate who you are, the closer you have moved toward wholeness. And from the perspective of wholeness, death is much easier to accept.

One of my clients had dramatic dreams that eventually brought him insights about his own fears and limitations.

Gilbert was a middle-aged professional who consulted me because he had a series of dreams that kept him from sleeping. He explained they all were about failing to perform well—failing a history test, being behind in tax payments, or missing a meeting at work. In these dream scenarios, his whole life was hinging on the outcome, and his agonizing question was, "Am I going to make it?" No wonder he couldn't fall back to sleep.

In his latest dream, he is driving a car up a mountain pass. He is his adult self. Sitting beside him in the passenger seat is a dark, shadowy figure wearing a black hoodie with a pointed tip at the crown, who never says a word or moves from his stationary position. He doesn't know who the passenger is, what he wants, or why he is riding along. The dream has other characters and actions that reflect back important information to him, but the shadow figure catches his attention the most.

Gilbert was ready to engage the energy of this character, even though he was frightening. After we worked with the parts of him that were strong and safe, he used his imagination to speak as the shadowy person. He said, "I'm Shadow Man, the dead part of Gilbert. I won't allow him to be with happy people [a key symbol in the dream] anymore—or a supportive community in his real life. The end of the road is near. Everything is dead from now on. There's no hope. My other name is Death, and I'm taking Gilbert away from all that was good in life."

Gilbert was shocked. He didn't realize he had a "dead part" in his psyche. Over the next months he went back to his dream to check in with Shadow Man and the other parts of his dream. We used the technique of Voice Dialogue along with dreamwork, which is very effective. He had filled three thick notebooks with dreams by the time they began to change and give him hope for a happier life.

Dream symbolism

It's very exciting to learn what dream symbols mean to the dreamer. Only she or he can correctly say what the image or action means. There are some universal symbols that tend to mean the same to most people—such as a house, which represents the self; or a circle, which usually represents wholeness. But there is always a personal association too; the lake that often is interpreted as spirituality or emotions can be seen as a place of terror to someone who almost drowned. Ultimately, the dreamer is the only expert interpreter of his or her dream symbology.

Sonny was so overwhelmed with his dream image of being covered by black, clawing birds—a prediction of his death, he believed—that he grasped at the symbolism of the raven in myth and story.

"The main thing is," he said, "apart from some of the creation stories, the raven is a predictor of death in almost every culture everywhere. There has to be something to it, then! In Europe, the Middle East, the Americas—*everywhere!*" He also was having many encounters with birds daily; they flew into the windows at work, perched on his head in the park, and flew around his car when he entered it.

Sonny had entered shadow land, and he needed me as a companion. I told him the story of the Morrigan, the Celtic goddess of death and rebirth. In the myths she is a shape-shifter, sometimes appearing as a mist, a thundercloud, or a dark horse carrying the soul of the dead, and at other times a hag hiding behind raven feathers. She comes to take the souls of the dead, and has control over which path that soul takes into rebirth. But she is primarily associated with death; in the myths she has a secret function known only to a few: guiding souls into the next birth.

Sonny asked to hear more myths about birds. I told him that some of the tribes I've been with see the bird as a special messenger who tells us it's time to go inward—to go into the dark, secluded place of incubation—into raven time. Its appearance in dreams announces that it's time for a psychological withdrawal from the outer world.

Amplifying your dream

Any work you do to expand the dream and work with the characters, objects, and events is active imagination. It helps them to reveal their deepest meaning to you. Active imagination in dreamwork also is fun and creative.

We did active imagination with the image of Sonny standing and covered by ravens. He reentered the dream, noticing all the details. Finally, in his imagination, he placed himself under the cover of the one hundred ravens, feeling the same fear he had in his dream when he was covered by the birds. After a while he breathed fast and hard.

"Oh, I'm not underneath anymore—the ravens are flying away, and instead of me, there's a large white crane! It's just standing there, still—a giant white crane! It's a whooping crane with black tips on its wings and a red spot on its forehead and cheeks. It's so beautiful. . . ."

I was quiet while he connected even more deeply to the imagery. After a few minutes, he came out of his light trance and looked at me with wonder. He shared that he felt energized, that working with the dream images had affected him deeply. He had a good feeling about the white crane, seeing it as a healing omen for his depression. "Everything is going to be okay," he said.

The next session he said he wanted to work more with the image of birds in general, and asked if I knew any more myths about them. Investigating myths about our dream symbols is another method of amplifying our dreams. The stories and themes expand our experience of our symbols and give us a wider base of understanding. Certain themes are universal, and since childhood, we have been primed to learn morals, cultural ideals, philosophies about life, and practical advice from stories. Stories, myths, and fables touch a depth of our consciousness that is beyond intellectual understanding. Through them, we are learning by metaphor rather than direct instruction, and some psychological theories state that metaphoric learning is more readily integrated into our psyches.

I told Sonny this story, found in the Basuto and Zulu tribes of Africa.

> A woman was gathering food for her family and encountered a wounded bird. She took it home and cared for it until it was healed. The bird began to give milk to the family, and so great was its output that everyone in the family scurried about for clay pots and sealed baskets to hold it. During the day the woman concealed the magical bird from the other villagers, and at night she brought it out to harvest its bounty. One day, her children, who were forbidden to

touch the bird, took it out into the forest to play with it and drink their fill of milk. They lost the bird, and tried to find it, without success. Suddenly, a storm of lightning and thunder came that was so violent, giant trees were uprooted and boulders rolled around like pebbles. An enormous bird appeared and covered the children with its wings, keeping them safe.

Afterward, the bird flew off with the children and raised them with care for many years, even putting them through their puberty rites at the proper time. When they had grown into young adults, the bird returned the children to their parents, and there was rejoicing and feasting in the village. The bird was gifted with many cattle, and from then on, the people and the bird were as family.

"I like that a lot," Sonny said. "I'd like to write a poem about that—the interdependence of humans and birds, or all animals. It's something I've thought about since I had the raven dream. Birds, ravens, crane, humans, me. The myth gives me hope again."

But he still insisted his dream was predicting his death from cancer, rejecting the possibility that it indicated death of parts of his psyche or phases of his life. He'd had a checkup that confirmed he was totally healthy. I congratulated Sonny on having the courage to work with difficult material, death and loss being the most difficult of all. When he addressed his fears in these areas, he discovered courage in himself that he had not known. He became a more confident person. Life became more peaceful for him, and he felt he could face any problem that came his way, including death. By doing dreamwork with his raven dream, he was able to release himself from the nightmare's grip.

Also, after working with the raven dream, he began to have dreams that embodied the opposite of fear and loss. They were dreams of inspiration and rebirth. He had made an internal shift. The following one that he shared with me had a mystical quality. He titled it "The Fountain."

Laughing, Sonny described an image of himself as an awkward twelve-year-old in faded red swim trunks, splashing in a fountain in the middle of town. This was forbidden, he said, and he could see a cop coming closer to apprehend him. The water shot upward out of the mouth of a dolphin sculpture, then cascaded down above his head, forming a shimmering room of water all around him. He felt invisible and invincible, even though he knew the policeman was approaching. "Guess that's what baptism is, a rebirth. And then we have the fountain of life—I was right in it. What a great dream this one is!" He said he would do active imagination with the dolphin fountain, placing himself in the shimmering room of water several times a day.

When we're ready to awaken, our inner wisdom creates a fountain and plunks us right down in the middle of it. The nature and miracle of consciousness is that it continually seeks transformation.

Another way to amplify your dream is by expressing it artistically.

Exercise: Make Dream Art

Most great artists are in touch with their dreams and visions and use them in their art. I know a woman who weaves the symbols of her dreams into shawls and scarves; the last one I saw depicted a complex story about flying to the stars and discovering a new breed of horses. Writers and filmmakers use characters and situations from their dreams in their creations. Use whatever medium pleases you—clay, written word, dance, painting, songwriting, sculpture, etc.—to express characters, objects, or events in your dream. You may also depict the feelings you had during the dream or afterward. Become as free as a child. Don't worry about being a good artist, singer, dancer, etc. This is personal expression for your own unfolding.

Symbolic dream interpretation

Sonny asked if we could interpret his raven dream symbolically, now that he had done his imaginative work. He had researched the symbolism of birds and read dream dictionaries and books that revealed exact meanings of dream symbols. Now he wanted me to share what I thought about his dream.

"I'll give it a try," I said, "but this isn't my normal way of doing dreamwork. I can't tell you what your dream means, but I'll tell you my associations. Since you've worked so well with it already, I'll associate to your meanings.

"The mist is a kind of heavenly elixir, mysterious and pervasive. Out of it fly birds, the symbol of the Holy Spirit, grace, or eternal life. Ancient Egyptian texts describe a person's ba as his eternal soul, depicted with the head of a bird and a human body. The multiplicity of birds shows the importance of the message. They are black, representing death or transformation. They have purpose and power, rising in spirals—representing the life cycle—from the sacred mist to the clear atmosphere, the heavens, where they are visible; you become aware of them. When they reach the zenith of flight, they turn and circle down to cover you. You are afraid you will be killed, signifying a major change. It's significant that there's movement from the earth to the heavens and back again by the birds, showing unification of these opposites. Birds cover you; you are buried in a cave or womb, to prepare for rebirth. There your dream ends, with you feeling the energy of transformation and the presence of the Holy Spirit. But it is incomplete—you are left in an incubatory state.

"When you did your piece of active imagination, you were reborn and became transformed from human into the white crane, pure spirit. At that moment you are holding the tension of the opposites of death and life: raven covering crane, black enveloping white. You stand still, and neither raven nor crane has flown away, so your ultimate nature—spiritual essence—remains nascent, and the transformation is not yet complete.

"Let's go back to your specific birds. Raven is both an ally and a destroyer. He lives by his cunning, boldly taking what he wants from us. In some countries he haunts the graveyards and pecks the corpses clean. In myths he is a trickster or shaman. He pecks open our psyches for treasure, pesters us out of our safety, and sometimes eats the parts of us that are no longer needed. In your dream he represents strong and quick transformation. The crane is known for his elaborate courtship dances, inviting an integration of the spiritual masculine and feminine energies within; the goal is their sacred marriage."

Whenever I'm asked to share my impressions, they come very quickly, and I know the thoughts for the first time as the words spill out. It's a process I trust, so I rarely censor anything.

But I felt I had talked too much, so I stopped. Sonny was appreciative, and said he would think about everything we'd discussed and see if he wanted to research his birds further. "It's a magnificent dream," I told him. "It's a great awakening for you and an announcement of a major change."

Although Sonny wanted my impressions and interpretation of his dream, you can develop the skill to do this for yourself with practice. Even just working with the images without interpretation can bring insights, wisdom, and psychological growth. Valuable learning occurs when working with a dream partner, even those at a beginning level of experience. Through commitment and practice, our skills in dreamwork develop. It's quite an adventure! You can further your knowledge of dreams with the resources at the end of the book, by working with a therapist, or by joining a dream group.

Sharing dreams

After you've worked on your dream by yourself, it's enriching to share it with someone you trust. You will know who will treat your dream with respect.

Exercise: Share Your Dream

In sharing your dreams, you are joining a lineage of ancestors from every culture, who have sat around the morning fire recounting their nightly dreams. Sharing dreams not only is psychologically healthy and creative; it opens us to the collective dreams of our community.

1. Find a trusted dream partner or a dream group with whom you can share your dreams on a regular basis. You can follow the format of the Elements of a Dream exercise described a few pages back, or agree on other methods of sharing. Wait until the dreamer has completed his or her work before offering suggestions or insights. Listen and support! Empower the dreamer to go more deeply into the dream. Even the simple act of telling the dream to someone brings it alive in the consciousness, giving one the opportunity to learn from it. Some dream groups continue for years with the same participants, revealing dream patterns and themes that weave through long periods of time.

2. Join an online website where you can contribute a dream and participate with other people to explore their dreams.

Children's dreams

Children love to share their dreams, and what better confidence builder than giving a child your full attention as she or he talks about what happened during a night adventure? Even though they may be mostly populated with cartoon characters, animals, or favorite story themes, their dreams show developmental processes that are important. And when the dreams are frightening, if parents just listen to the dream, it comforts the child.

Children who are at the end of their lives tend to have very direct dreams about their death. An angel will come in a dream to announce that they will be going to heaven the next day, or a relative who has died will say he's coming to take the child on a big trip. The children I've worked with generally are comforted and matter-of-fact about these dreams, and aren't upset until they see their parents' reactions to the dream.

One girl, Mattie, had been in a children's cancer ward for eight months. Her dreams were amazing in their detail, and she enjoyed drawing and painting them, and acting out the voices of the dream characters—mostly animals. As she weakened and it became apparent her body couldn't survive, she reported that the animal family in her dreams was very tired, and they were sleeping all the time. The last time I visited her, she had dreamed that her animals needed her and she wanted to go to them and lie down with them. She passed away the next day. Her mother sent me a photo of her last crayon drawing, in which she lay with her arms embracing a dog and a pig, surrounded by other sleeping animals.

Dream incubation

It is possible to seed your unconscious with a question, problem, or subject before you go to sleep by requesting a dream about it. Or you can ask your inner wisdom to present you with a dream that elucidates another dream you've had. You can request a new dream about a dream character or about the previous dream as a whole.

You may then wake up in the morning with a dream that addresses your request. It takes practice and patience to reap the rewards of dream incubation, but I've found that people who practice the technique for a few weeks usually get positive results. Even if it appears that your dream is not a specific answer to your request, you can trust that the material that came is worthwhile. And it may be more related to your incubation than is apparent at first.

Exercise: Incubate a Dream

1. Place your dream journal and a pen on the nightstand next to your bed. Have the journal open to a blank page.

2. Before you lie down to sleep, sit on the edge of the bed with both feet flat on the floor. Close your eyes. Relax your body. Take four or five deep breaths.

3. Say silently or out loud, "I'm ready to receive a dream about _____." Examples of things you may want to dream about include which job to take, your shyness, what's causing your anxiety, how to share more from your heart, or the next step in a creative project. You can ask to receive further information about a dream or dream symbol you've already worked with. Make the statement direct and simple.

4. Repeat the statement at least four times, or until you feel you have planted the suggestion in your unconscious.

5. Lie down and get ready for sleep. Repeat the statement a few more times with your eyes closed.

6. If you want to try a modified Tibetan technique, visualize gentle blue energy at your throat as you say or think your statement lying down. This activates the

throat center, which is involved in communication and dreaming, along with the forehead energy center.

7. Go to sleep.

8. When you awaken, write down your dream.

9. Work with your dream now or later, using the previous exercises.

10. Thank your unconscious for responding to your request.

11. Practice incubating a dream the next night and continue the practice, using the same intentional statement or a different one.

Months after I last had seen him, I had a message from Sonny on my answering machine that said, "There's a dragon breathing down my neck, and it isn't a dream. Call me, please." He had consulted his physician because he didn't feel well. After many blood tests, imaging, and finally a liver biopsy, he was diagnosed with advanced cirrhosis of the liver. His health had deteriorated quickly, leaving him debilitated and discouraged. He was told he needed a liver transplant.

"Remember my raven dream, Carolyn?" he said when I met with him. "If I get sicker before I get a transplant, I'll die. That's what the dream was about."

He was ready to discuss the possibility of death. Although he feared abandoning his family, the same fear he first revealed with his raven dream when we began our work, he said he wouldn't mind dying because he knew he would go to God and have an existence in the afterlife. "I'll just miss my wife and holding my little gremlins," he said, "but I'm sure I can watch over them from the other side." He shed a few tears, and then talked more about his faith.

Before I could visit him again, Sonny called. His voice was raspy, and he said it was uncomfortable to talk, but he wanted to tell me a dream. "It was short. At first I thought I was seeing the crane again, but it wasn't a bird. It was an angel, with tremendous, snow-white wings. The soft feathers at the tip of her wings—it was a woman—touched me on the forehead as I was lying in bed. She said I was going to die, and there was nothing to fear. Then she disappeared. I can't explain how I feel: a kind of comfort and peace, and a bit curious. I can't believe I'm saying this. Should I tell my wife?" I answered that this was an important discussion to have with her, no matter how painful it might be, and if the dream were not announcing his physical death, it still would be an intimate, valuable sharing.

Five days later, his wife phoned me late at night. She was crying and told me Sonny had died an hour earlier of a heart attack. "When the pain got worse, he looked in my eyes and said, 'Good-bye, my love.' He went quickly."

The family grieved easily and fully. They said Sonny had shared his angel dream with them and with his children as well. He told them that he always would be protecting them.

When they came to my office the next day, his six-year-old daughter turned to me and said brightly, "Daddy's in heaven now. He's dead, actually." Her younger brother added, "Yeah. And we can't see him for a long, long time, and we'll miss him, but we get to be with him later. In heaven." They waved good-bye and turned to leave the room, grasping their mother's hands.

Sonny and I had been on a rich journey together. I admired

his willingness to go deep into an exploration of his psyche and his life; his commitment to do the dreamwork was steadfast. All his dreams were extraordinary in their presentation of mythic symbols and meanings, demonstrating the transformational power of inner work. And he faced his death with courage and trust. It made me happy that he shared his dreams of the birds and his angel with his family—he included his wife and children in his dying process in the most intimate way. I realized that I too would miss him.

Practicing dreamwork is one of the most profound ways we can initiate personal transformation. Whether you are a veteran dream explorer or a beginner, activate your dream practice by doing the exercises in this chapter. When you interact with your dreams and treat them as the lively entities they are, they respond accordingly, guiding you further toward your wholeness.

CHAPTER 11

Celebrate Your Life

The metaphysical mystery, thus recognized by common sense, that he who feeds on death that feeds on men possesses life supereminently and excellently, and meets best the secret demands of the universe . . .

—William James, *The Varieties of Religious Experience*

We all know people who, as they near the end of their lives, announce that they don't want a funeral, but want a celebration of their lives instead. I heard of one woman who wanted to make sure her celebration was as audacious as a celebrity's party, so she hired an event planner and arranged a carnival for her whole small town to attend. It was a day of Ferris wheel rides, free cotton candy and hot dogs, circus acts, and neighbors enjoying themselves. Off to the side of the festivities was a small white tent that was set up as a chapel, where people could mourn and pay their respects to her ashes. Perhaps this seems extravagant, but it's an example of the many creative ways people choose to honor their lives.

Make a life review

We also have a desire to honor ourselves internally—to find meaning in our existence as we complete our lives. *The arc of a human life is the most beautifully intricate art form.* From the complexities of our family structure, our environment, and our physical and mental characteristics, to the random and not-so-random events and choices we encounter, we weave the extraordinary tapestry that is our life. Almost everyone has one central question at the end: What has been meaningful? Have we spent our time on earth wisely? What would we do differently if we could do it over? These inquiries are soul work. Connecting to the meaning of our life brings us into wholeness, making it easier to let go and transition into death.

John, a client of mine, said he was depressed—not about his impending death, but by the fact that when he was gone nothing of him would be left for his children and grandchildren. He said his belongings and savings didn't count, because they had nothing to do with who he was.

He wanted to leave a legacy.

So even though he didn't feel well, with my encouragement, he spent an hour each morning recording stories about his life that he wanted his family to know. He was a perfectionist, and attacked the project with every ounce of energy he had, even using two tape recorders so his family would have a duplicate set. When his grandchildren visited, they loved listening to his storytelling and helping with the recordings. After several weeks and many boxes of tapes and batteries, he reported that he was no longer depressed. "I'm really enjoying revisiting my past," he told me, "and now I can leave in peace." John and others have received comfort and a sense of satisfaction from immersing themselves in their personal stories. Sharing in this way is most effective when you talk about which people and events and accomplishments were the most meaningful. When shared with others, the stories of one's life become valuable teachings.

You may not be as interested in reviewing your life as John was. Perhaps you need to concentrate your energy on getting through each day now, or you've already released your past and are more focused on your transition into death or the afterlife. That's a valid choice. Take a moment of quiet now to check inside and see if you have even a small desire to look over your life. I guarantee that whether or not you share your life stories with others, even a minimal evaluation of what you've lived and learned can bring emotional resolution and a new understanding of what your experiences have meant.

It's never too late for transformation. By engaging in a review of your life you have the opportunity to resolve personal conflicts and appreciate past actions and parts of yourself that you've ignored. It's a chance to open into healing states and actualize into wholeness. And it's an opportunity to celebrate and give thanks for your unique life.

We will explore several types of life review in this chapter. Telling stories is practiced in tribes all over the world through dance, art, ritual, chant, and spoken word. Storytelling is used to record tribal history, such as when the Inuit hunters of the past would recount their successful whale hunt by chanting and dancing the day's events to the whole village. In the modern world it's expressed through memoir, poetry, theater, documentary film, blogging, etc. It is the most basic and engaging form of communication.

Exercise: Share Your Stories

1. Plan to make an audio or video recording of yourself telling the stories of your life, your philosophy, and what you've learned. You can ask someone to help you. You may want to invite your family or others to the live storytelling session as you record it, which makes it a joyful occasion as well as your legacy. Afterward, allow time for your audience to comment and ask questions, so your sharing becomes interactive.

2. You may choose to privately create a journal filled with your stories and drawings, or you may want to use a computer. You might even prefer to silently review the progression of your life stories by just thinking about them. In any case, know that the memories and insights will flow once you begin.

3. Remember, what you take for granted can be a treasure for others. Just start sharing, taking yourself back to earlier times. Include the *important events and people in your life*. Describe *what you would like to do if you had the chance*. You do not need to tell your stories in order, but some of you will find it easier to start from the beginning of your life. Go with whatever comes into your mind first. Describe all the details as you remember them—they add vitality to your storytelling.

4. Enjoy the process of revealing how your life has unfolded. Everyone is a natural storyteller. Give up any need to present yourself as a perfect person—just tell the truth as you remember it, and your story will be meaningful to your audience. Emphasize the lessons you've learned, and share your viewpoints, wisdom,

and advice. Send your inner critic off to the beach and
have fun!

I had a client who changed his life dramatically before he
died because of the life review we did. His name was Marco.
He was forty-two when he contracted multiple sclerosis, a disease in which there is damage to the myelin sheaths around the
neurons of the spinal cord and brain, leaving them unable to
communicate with one another. He had been a successful stock-
broker and self-proclaimed "swinging bachelor," who valued
expensive clothes and his sports car above all.

"It sucks that I can't do the things I used to anymore," he told
me, "but I realize I'm happy not to be working anymore. I
thrived on the competition and loved the rewards, but now that
I'm home all day, it's great not being under pressure." Marco
was a strongly opinionated man who saw himself as a person
with exceptional power. I knew from previous experience that
people who are in touch only with their power side experience
considerable distress when their illness brings up their vulnerability. Often they become depressed or even self-destructive.
After six sessions, he chose to terminate our work together because he didn't find it helpful.

Ten years later, I received a message from Sofia, Marco's
caretaker, saying he wanted to see me. She led me into Marco's
bedroom, which looked like a hospital room, complete with
electric bed and elaborate medical equipment that beeped and
clicked. His face was swollen and smooth—from cortisone, Sofia said. His eyes were open, and it seemed they were pleading
with me desperately. He didn't speak.

Sofia explained that he was totally paralyzed, except for his eyes and a few muscles in his face. A breathing machine was secured to his tracheotomy; it was operating for all but a few hours a day. With the respiratory machine's hose hooked into his throat, he was unable to speak. And when he wasn't connected to the breathing machine he still couldn't talk because he had a neurological disorder called "dysarthria," which affects a person's ability to articulate words. So he communicated by using a special computer for those who can't speak. By moving his eyes as he looked at the terminal, he could bring up a selection of screens on the device; each screen displayed icons and statements pertinent to his needs, such as:

I need to be changed.
I'm hungry.
Close the curtains. I want to sleep.
Thank you.

When he indicated each icon or written sentence with his eye movements, a clear voice spoke the words, sentences, or phrases. The assistive device also gave him control over his TV and was a fully functioning computer. For expression of words or phrases that were not programmed into the device, there was a screen of the alphabet to spell out a message, which was then voiced.

When I approached his bed, tears rolled down his face. Sofia told me he was slow in using the assist, so I should be patient for his responses. Then she left the room.

His eyes moved quickly. "Three years," the device announced.

"You've been like this three years?" I asked.

"Yes." There was a long pause as he looked to his left, right, and other directions. I could see him spelling on the alphabet screen, the chosen letters popping up and forming words below. There were several accidental substitutions of neighboring letters, but the sentences were readable.

"I need help understand my life," the device suddenly said in a staccato voice. "I want live msny yeard. Even like this. Doctor surprised I'm still alove. Why this happen? Why was I born? I wasted my life."

I was touched by the intensity of his searching, which was transmitted through the mechanical voice and typewritten sentences. How could we converse about these philosophical matters that were important to him, given his slow and abbreviated utterances? Just begin, I thought, and we'll see what happens.

The questions he was asking could lead him into a deep exploration that is particularly valuable to people facing death. To see the arc of one's life and the patterns that have played through is a starting point for transformation. As difficult and slow as it would be, I decided that the best way to address Marco's questions would be by doing a guided life review.

I prepared myself for Marco's life review. Given the challenge of his need to use the speech assistive device, I wasn't sure that it would go smoothly. But I knew that reviewing one's life through remembered images and feelings usually brings an appreciation of what we've accomplished, endured, and learned, as well as an expression of remorse and redemption. To see the overview of one's life is a starting point for transformation. He responded well when I guided him into a review of his early life. He was able to visualize well and seemed pleased with the experience. I decided that it would require sessions over a period of two weeks to do what I usually guided people through in an hour.

I played slow ambient music to help him relax. I asked him to remember how it felt to float on his back in a swimming pool, letting the warm water support him and the sun warm his belly. "Keep all your attention on these feelings and sensations," I said, "and let your mind drift away. If thoughts enter, they are just guests passing by. Listen to the sound of the water lapping onto your body. Enjoy that sound." I was surprised how readily he was inducted by my voice and the music into an altered state, shown by his rapid eye movements, which indicated he was having imagery.

I guided him into memories of his first five years, encouraging details about environment, people around him, and specific events. I invited him to experience the feelings he had then, the concerns and joyful times. His child's view of loving parents and jealousy when his siblings were born were the most vivid and emotional memories he talked about afterward. He shared his wonder at the small, anxious boy he had been. "The hard parts of life made me strong," the device announced. And then I saw him choose a happy-face icon on the screen.

You may prefer a more structured method of reviewing your life, rather than the free-form sharing of your life stories as in the previous exercise. If so, here is a detailed script for you to use.

Exercise: Guided Life Review Script

This exercise requires the help of someone you trust—a friend, a spiritual adviser, a sponsor, maybe your therapist. Pick a quiet place where you won't be interrupted, and allow about an hour so you'll have plenty of time to share afterward. You may want to record the sharing part of your session at the end, so have a digital recorder set up and ready to go. Put on some meditative music, such as one of the selections I've suggested in the Resources section.

The person guiding you is a trusted ally who will facilitate and witness your experience. An intuitive connection will develop between you and your guide when he or she focuses on your breathing. Once the two of you are energetically connected, you will go deeper into this hypnotic state. Your guide will soon sense how long to pause in between statements. Here is a complete life review script to follow if you choose. It is designed to be completed in one session, but because it is somewhat lengthy, you may take a break in the middle if you need to. Or, you and your guide can create a similar format of your own choosing.

1. Lie down or sit comfortably. Close your eyes. Have your journal nearby, open to blank pages, and a pen.

2. Your friend, who is guiding you, will sit nearby and will operate the music player and the recorder.

3. Your friend starts the music, keeping it at a soft volume.

4. Friend **slowly** and quietly reads this script: *Inhale deeply from your belly, and let out the air as slowly as you can . . . even more slowly. . . . Do this seven times. Let go of any tension in your jaw, shoulders, and belly. . . .* Friend counts the breaths silently. When you have completed six breaths, friend says: *When you are finished, breathe normally. . . . Good . . . continue to relax and let go. . . . All the events of your life are stored in your*

memory, in full detail. . . . All you need to do . . . is ask for them to be replayed. . . . You will experience thoughts . . . feelings . . . and images . . . at my suggestion.

5. Friend: *Invite your wisdom to present you with an image and feeling of a home you lived in between birth and twelve years of age. Take your time. Look around and see what room or yard you are in. . . . You are in this place now. . . . Notice all the details.* (Pause for about thirty seconds.) *Go to a place or object and touch it, feeling its texture, color, and shape. . . . Good.* (Pause)

6. Friend: *Look down at your body . . . notice what you are wearing. . . . How old are you? How do you feel? . . . Move around . . . feel your body moving.*

7. Friend: *Now look around and see who else is in your home. Perhaps you are sitting together with your family at the dinner table. . . . See all the details in the scene . . . look at everyone there.* (Pause for thirty seconds.) *Who does your attention rest on? . . . Ask that person if they have something to say to you, and listen for the response.* (Pause for thirty seconds.) *Good . . . who would you like to give you a hug? . . . Go to that person . . . feel the touch of their body . . . notice how you feel. . . . Good.*

When you are ready, you can go anywhere you wish, as yourself at any age between birth and twelve years old. Let the memories come and notice all the details and feelings. Take your time. Raise your index finger when you are finished. . . . Good. . . . Know that you can come back here at any time. . . . For now, imagine that you are looking at a clear blue sky with white shapes . . . feel their lightness and beauty. (Pause for thirty seconds.)

8. Friend: *Yes. . . . Ask your wisdom now to present you with a scene or event in your life between the ages of thirteen*

and twenty-one. . . . Accept anything at all that comes . . . don't censor. . . . See the images, feel the feelings . . . all the details. . . . Take your time. . . . Signal with your finger when you are finished.

9. Friend: *Now again imagine you are looking at the blue sky . . . notice the shape of the clouds. . . . It feels good to remember people, events, and feelings from your past.*

10. Friend repeats number 8, using the ages **twenty-two to thirty**.

11. Friend repeats number 8 using the ages **thirty-one to forty-five**.

12. Friend continues repeating number 8 in increments of fifteen years to the present.

13. Friend: *Good work. . . . Remember, you can come back to any of these ages you may want to explore further. . . . For now . . . it's time to complete. . . . See the blue sky and the clouds again . . . all your attention there. . . .* (Pause for thirty seconds.)

14. Friend: *Feel the [floor, chair, couch, etc.] beneath you now. . . . Bring your awareness to the present. . . .* (Talk at normal speed now.) *Feel your body. Notice your breathing. Open your eyes now, fully present. Feeling good.* Friend gradually turns off music, dialing down the volume slowly.

15. When you are ready, share your experiences with your friend. If you want your conversation recorded, turn on the machine. Take your time to talk about your **thoughts, feelings, insights, and images**. Talk about what you learned and what you would do differently. Decide if you need to make amends to anyone. Share which experiences were meaningful to you

and how you've helped others. Talk about any attitudes or viewpoints you want to change. Your friend can prompt you with the age ranges, or ask questions. Or you may prefer to be alone and write about your experience in your journal.

16. Afterward, write in your journal any questions or aspects of your review you wish to explore further. You probably will have additional memories you want to write about.

When you are finished, make sure you are fully grounded. Drinking water or eating fruit is helpful because it activates the body and brings energy down from your head. Walk around before driving.

Returning to Marco's story, his family was becoming worn out from taking care of him and responding to his many demands. I saw him insist that his mother read a Dean Koontz novel to him even though she wasn't feeling well. She gave in when the machine announced, "I need it!" At times they were honest among themselves when they weren't with Marco, about wanting him to die soon. They didn't understand why he wanted to live, because he didn't have quality of life. But they loved him and tried to please him.

How could Marco's parents and siblings feel this way? The stress of caring for a severely disabled person is enormous. There is also a great deal of projection about how they would feel in Marco's condition; they imagine he would want to die soon in order to avoid suffering. None of this was true for Marco. Even when his family talked to him about their struggles, he blocked out the obvious stress they were experiencing regarding his wish for daily visits and constant attention. He did not want to "go gentle into that good night," and adapted to his paralyzed state. His demands were an attempt to maintain personal power; he was fighting to stay alive. The demands also signified his regression to an infantile state, which sometimes happens with severely ill people who feel they are losing everything. I felt compassion for Marco and his family. They were locked in a dance that stripped everyone down to raw emotions and conflicting values.

One problem Marco presented to his parents was his refusal to tell them what he wanted for his death. They were Jewish and hoped he would want a traditional service and burial. But he wouldn't talk about it when they gingerly brought up the subject.

Regain energy from the past

Another person who benefited from doing a life review was a ninety-five-year-old woman named Martha, whom I worked with. Initially she was very quiet and cooperative as I inducted her into the process, which we recorded. She was interested in providing a modest account of her life, told in story form from her memories, as a legacy for her family. As the memories and insights began to come alive for her, her whole personality changed. She became animated and expressive, laughing and enjoying the youthful escapades she described. "I was a wild one!" she exclaimed. "It's great to remember things I forgot!" She was grateful for the vitality she regained, and her family had the treasure of her stories in their hearts and minds to pass on to following generations.

I had a fourteen-year-old client, Georgia, who was nearing death because of a failing heart. Her spirits were high even though she knew the end was near. She wanted to think about the meaning of her short life, and spontaneously began sharing what she'd learned, what she would miss, and what "the beautiful parts" were. She wasn't afraid. She chose to record her life in detail through video, so "some part of me will always be alive." Interestingly, the time period she focused on the most was when she was seven years old, a time when she felt the most free to be herself. As Georgia spoke about playing on the swing in the park at that age and dressing her dolls, she said these happy memories filled her with hope and took away her physical pain. Perhaps the act of remembering positive experiences produces mood-enhancing chemicals in the brain.

Reclaim an unlived life

When we are contemplating the completion of our lives, it is natural to wonder about the things we wish we had done, or places we would have liked to visit, or experiences we feel we missed out on. One man I worked with, Abe, had regrets about never having the courage to take time from his work to walk through the jungles of Guatemala. He didn't remember where the idea came from—perhaps a childhood book or movie—but he wanted to hike and canoe through the thick jungle to Mayan ruins that had been excavated. He often had dreams of astronomical hieroglyphs that he felt were Mayan.

He was too ill to make the trip physically, so he gathered together guidebooks and maps and planned his theoretical trip. Years before, I had led a traveling seminar to the ruins he was particularly interested in, so I had contacts in the area. Once Abe had his trip planned in detail and had viewed documentaries of the ruins, we phoned the tour guide company I had used. Abe had a list of questions a mile long, and he and the guide enjoyed a wonderful conversation. "I was there as he described everything!" he said. A week later he received a package of personal photos the guide had taken of the ruins, along with translations of some Mayan prayers about the continuity of life. Abe decided he wanted the photos and prayers to be shared at his memorial celebration.

Recently, a hospice representative brought me up-to-date with some of the unique services her hospice provides. She told me about a female resident who was 102 years old. The woman was cheerful all the time, even though she was debilitated and nearing the end of her life. When she was guided in a life review, her regret was that she had never taken a ride in a hot air balloon. She wanted to feel the wind and the freedom of drifting over the landscape in a basket. All the hospice volunteers and friends pooled their resources and made special arrangements for her to have her balloon ride. The photos the representative showed me were amazing—an exuberant tiny woman waving at the world, high in the clouds. It was a wonderful example of how friends and family can celebrate someone's final wishes.

Another friend of mine, Tonia, who lives on a farm in Alberta, Canada, decided to create a new tradition for her family for generations to come. She is in the end stages of cancer, and last Christmas she announced to her many relatives that from now on, she would offer any family member who got married her cherished wineglasses and carafe to make a wedding toast— items she had saved for her own wedding, which never happened. The photo she sent me displayed two exquisitely cut crystal goblets and an elegant wine pitcher standing on a silken cloth. Furthermore, to have her nieces and nephews participate in her funeral celebration, she has asked them to decorate the top of her handmade coffin with painted flowers. And to please herself, painted on the inside of her coffin will be a sunset.

Think of ways you would enjoy celebrating your life and leaving a legacy. Be as creative as you wish—this is your life. You may imagine yourself in your personal sanctuary that you created in the exercise in chapter nine; petition your inner wisdom to present you with thoughts, images, and feelings about how you could celebrate your life.

Create an event

Sometimes people want to celebrate their lives by doing something meaningful for others. When they are feeling well, they help young people or those less fortunate. One man gathered job trainees from an addiction recovery center and invited them into his home. After a backyard barbecue, he held a mentoring session about how to apply for a job and be a successful employee. He talked about discipline, interview skills, and having the proper attitude. Afterward, he gave his suits and most of his clothes to them. The men learned a lot and enjoyed themselves. Our mentor felt that he had done something beneficial by passing on his knowledge.

A client of mine wanted to do something for the environment

before he died. He was a camping enthusiast who kept a journal of all the national parks he had visited in this country and Canada. His goal was to get young people more directly connected to nature. "Before I get too weak," he said, "I've got to do something. I should have taken action years ago. I want to put my last bit of energy into a worthwhile project." He had the means to donate money to existing organizations, he said, but wanted to do something hands-on. He got in touch with a Boy Scout troop leader and arranged to lead the boys in a project of planting trees. He taught them how to care for seedlings and the proper way to put them into the earth. The boys earned a badge for their project, and their mentor fulfilled his heartfelt goal.

The inclination to serve others during the last phase of life is a natural celebration and expression of gratitude. Even if you have fear or sadness about leaving this earth, it feels satisfying and right to give to others. One woman said to me after she found out she didn't have long to live, "Well, I know my job now. It's to give away everything I own and everything I am. Give, give, give."

Another practice that is becoming more common is to have a "living funeral." This celebration can take any form. It can be a large party or a small gathering of loved ones at the bedside. The person being honored says good-bye publicly or privately to each guest. One person I know wanted dancing and a band. Another wanted the celebration to be in a fancy restaurant in a private room, so medical transport was arranged and a nurse stayed with my client as he lay on a gurney at the head of the table. He wore a tuxedo jacket and frilly white shirt over his pajama bottoms. His upper body was elevated so he could converse with his guests. He even took a few sips of champagne and made a humorous speech.

You may think these are extreme celebrations, but they were meaningful for those who carried them out. And what fun to go against tradition! Finally, at the end of your life, you can be free to do something wild.

Exercise: Make an Ethical Will

Writing an ethical will is another way to celebrate your life. As you consider dispersing your property to family and friends in your last will and testament, it's equally if not more important to give your life's values, experience, and wisdom to your loved ones. The tradition of writing an ethical will dates back to biblical days. It is a unique, creative expression of who you are, what you believe and know, and the hopes and desires you have for those who will miss you when you are gone. It is not a legal document. Ethical wills are a meaningful part of family history, and have been passed down through generations.

Often an ethical will is read at a memorial service. Or it may be a private communication to a son or daughter, community group, or a business that was owned by the deceased. I have seen families find comfort and closeness when the writer of the will shares it out loud—it can be shared at any time in the writer's life. I have a friend who wrote hers after the birth of her first child, addressing it to her baby. I'm thinking of writing one that also contains advice for my niece about practical matters such as buying a home. It can be in any form; the following is just a sample.

1. Begin to write what's important to you in all areas of your life. Keep in mind whom you are addressing. Write naturally, as you speak. Talk about:

   - your values

   - your spiritual beliefs

   - your philosophy of how to relate to others

   - mottoes or guidelines you live by

   - your feelings about each person you are addressing

   - your hopes and advice for each person

   - what you are sorry to be leaving behind

   - what you appreciate in your life

   - anything else you wish, like a poem or blessing

2. Arrange a gathering to celebrate the reading of your ethical will. You may want to play music or have a picnic or a potluck dinner. Even if it is held at the side of your bed, you set the tone of celebration. One of my clients who was bedridden had a friend invite the important people in her life to come together in her bedroom. She asked her family and friends to take turns reading her ethical will aloud, since she was too ill to read it herself. Her first sentence was, "I want this to be a celebration of my life—not a sad time."

_____

We were nearing the end of Marco's life review. As we progressed through the stages of his life over the two weeks, his personality softened. His family reported that he made fewer demands and began to show interest in how their lives were going, instead of just focusing on himself. During our final session of the process, tears ran down his face as the music ended.

Marco experienced huge changes in his life over a relatively short period of time. Because he was addicted to success both at work and in his personal life, his physical deterioration and new dependence on others represented a move from one end of the power/vulnerability continuum to the other. His relentless, unkind demands of Sofia, his helper, and of his family, cruel as they seemed, were born of an attempt to regain the sense of power that he had enjoyed.

However, once we had completed our review of his life, in which Marco was able to remember and discover meaningful experiences, his personality changed. He found value in the knowledge that he was loved and had been well supported by his parents while growing up. He developed an appreciation for all that they and Sofia had done for him during the years he had been ill. He finally recognized the sacrifices they had made to care for him.

Part of our life review was to heal the unfinished business he had with himself and others, which he then bravely addressed. He was able to forgive himself for the attitudes and actions that had been self-destructive and damaging to his relationships. The other important shift Marco experienced in his review, which enabled him to soften and open to love even more, was when he could recognize the good he had contributed to the world over his lifetime. His relationship with himself became fuller, incorporating all of who he was. He spoke of "living a good life." This new vision of himself in the world allowed him to treat those around him with a newfound sense of respect.

The last time I went to visit, Marco's father told me he was sleeping. When I entered his room, I noticed a rattling sound in his chest. I checked with Sofia and she said the nurse had suctioned him twice that day as usual. I told her to call the agency and have a nurse come again. The nurse examined him and reported that Marco had pneumonia and was still sleeping. I advised the family that people on respirators are more susceptible to pneumonia, and that it often ends their lives, so they should stay nearby.

The next morning when I arrived the whole family was present. The morning nurse had said he was dying, and that it would happen soon. They had called their rabbi, who notified the congregation to have everyone pray for Marco. The family had been praying also. I entered Marco's room alone and sat by his bed. From the jerky movements of his closed eyes, I sensed he was agitated. His raspy, uneven breathing came with effort. I told him that when he was ready, he could let go, that everything was happening as it was supposed to. He could relax, because soon his suffering would be over. As I finished the last sentence, his eyes popped open; he was looking at me, but I knew he didn't see me.

"Come now," I said to the family and Sofia. "He's leaving."

All gathered around his bed, touching him. Prayers were said. His mother lay down next to him on the bed and sobbed. His eye movements stopped. The nurse checked for a pulse and turned off the respirator.

❧

As you share your life stories with others or do the scripted life review, you may be surprised at the patterns that emerge.

Hopefully, you will appreciate all that you have endured and learned and will have a newfound or refreshed compassion for the beautiful being you are. Celebrate your accomplishments and the goodness you have brought to the world. When you realize that your life has been meaningful, you are moving toward wholeness.

Afterword

From the middle of life onward, only he remains
vitally alive who is ready to *die with life*. For in the
secret hour of life's midday the parabola is reversed, death is born.

—C. G. Jung, "The Soul and Death"

Fear of death is wired into our brains from birth as the basic
instinct of self-preservation. In the previous chapters we've
experienced the journeys of many of my friends and clients who
were able to transcend this fear, not only accepting their impending deaths but also embracing the end of their lives fully, as
part of a whole life. The beauty they found in death demon-
strates how the goal at the end of life is not merely to receive
palliative care and eliminate fear, but to facilitate our personal
growth during the time we have left. Thus you can complete
what you experience as unfinished, awaken the parts of yourself
that were nascent, and enter into a feeling of wholeness and peace.

Abraham Maslow says it well:

All the evidence that we have indicates that it is reasonable to assume in practically every human being,
and certainly in almost every newborn baby, that
there is an active will toward health, an impulse towards growth, or towards actualization.

This impulse toward growth, I believe, accelerates when we become aware that we have an especially limited time on this earth. Most of the people I've worked with grab onto the opportunity for personal transformation and are eager to seek completion at the end of their lives. I use the word *grab* because that's what it feels like to me when they respond with such enthusiasm— which isn't always the case when it comes to personal growth work! Initially, I thought their excitement about the process was born of a need to do something while they awaited death, but I've learned that it's in fact a person's drive toward actualization that propels them into this final inner exploration.

I remember talking with a friend who knew he would die within a few weeks from inoperable lung cancer. I commented on his happiness. He said, "Here we are, outside by the ocean, with good friends and family, feeling the sun and looking one another in the eyes. It's a great day. It's really all we have— today. Why shouldn't I be happy?" He had enjoyed the life review we had done earlier, and felt that his life was in order and complete. We had marveled at all that he had experienced during his lifetime. "I am in love with life," he said, "no matter how long it lasts."

At this time in our history, our culture is focused on how to remain youthful, not on how to prepare for death. The aging process is seen as an enemy we must battle; we don't think of death as a natural end to our life cycle—certainly not a desirable one. This attitude costs us a great deal of suffering when our time to depart arrives. Anyone fifty years of age or older should consider Jung's epigraph at the head of this chapter: "the secret hour of life's midday," when "death is born." We don't need to wait until we are terminally ill to take the opportunity to consider the end of our cycle, to transform into a truer version of who we are.

Most indigenous cultures are far more accepting of death than is Western culture. In some cultures, death is celebrated rather than being hidden or denied. A friend of mine, Miguel Rivera, calls himself a minister and an intercessor. Born in Guatemala, he leads ceremonial sweat lodges, vision quests, and coming-of-age rituals for young people and adults here in the United States. He also ministers to people who are dying. "One thing I do is sing to them," he says. "Ceremonial prayer songs that are Native American or Yoruban, or from anywhere. I sing and sing. The songs help people relax and move the energy from the head all the way to the feet. And I ask them, 'Are you done? Are you finished with your life?' And if they're not, we talk about what needs to be done."

Miguel explains that in his community, people are less likely to be afraid of death because they know it's not a lonely place. The living are intimately connected to their ancestors in the spirit world. There is reciprocity between the two worlds, and this reciprocal relationship is honored through ritual and prayer at the family altar in the home. In this way, the departed are very much alive. Once the dead are integrated into the larger cycle of life, this sense of always belonging, of a never-ending connection to loved ones, eliminates fear. People feel related to all beings on the earth. When someone picks an ear of corn, he or she will tell the plant, "I will be food for your relatives when I go into the earth." In this culture, respect and a sense of reciprocity are expressed to all plants and animals. Death is faced head-on. Children know their grandfather is dying, and climb with ease onto their *abuelo*'s bed to coax yet another story from him about the ancestors, and to request that he visit soon once he has passed on.

I believe children should be judiciously included when a family member is dying. Depending on their age, explanations of death can be shared with children in simple ways, or with more complex details if they are older. We should take care not to overload a child with more information than he or she can handle. In my experience, it is harmful to try to cloak death and the dying process in complete secrecy to protect a child. Children are intuitive and bright, sensing that something important is happening. Whispers and secrecy create anxiety and mistrust for young ones, causing more harm than good. My hope is that our children learn that death is a natural part of life.

According to some futurists, death may be quite different in the next fifty to one hundred years. In his book *The Singularity Is Near*, Ray Kurzweil states that biotechnology and nanotechnology will become so advanced, and our interdependence with these technologies will become so entwined, that our bodies and brains will have the power to heal and recover from almost any disease or injury. Illness and suffering will be relegated to such a minor part of our lives that we will be healthy for our entire time on this earth. We will even be able to reverse the aging process. Life extension will become not only possible, but the norm. Kurzweil says we might be able to live forever, or until we choose to end our lives.

Does this sound like science fiction? The 2012 Nobel Prize in Physiology or Medicine indicates that we are headed in this direction. It was granted to Sir John Gurdon and Shinya Yamanaka for their joint discovery that "mature, specialized cells can be reprogrammed to become immature cells capable of developing into all tissues of the body." This revolutionary discovery means that embryonic-like stem cells can be created in the laboratory from adult cells of the same organism. The ability to reprogram cells suggests future medical treatments that have been impossible until now. New cells, created in the laboratory, will be able to replace cells damaged by disease. The implications are mind-boggling.

But for now we have the personal and social problems of how to face and prepare for death. If you are in this position, I hope these stories of my friends and clients as well as the exercises in this book will inspire you to begin or deepen your journey of inner work. And if you are privileged to guide a person who is dying, my wish is that you both reap the benefits of entering into the explorations I suggest.

It is a blessing to face death from a place of wholeness and a full heart. Whether you are close or far from "the great cold that surrounds your bones," as the character Data describes death in an episode of *Star Trek: The Next Generation*, I invite you to join me in practicing these principles of wholeness:

- Be yourself
- Be present
- Open to unconditional love and compassion
- Be of service to others
- Make each day meaningful
- Live in gratitude

And then, when it is time for the end-of-life passage we must all take, we can be like the ones David Whyte so beautifully describes in this excerpt from his poem "Sometimes."

Sometimes
if you move carefully
through the forest,

breathing
like the ones
in the old stories,

who could cross
a shimmering bed of leaves
without a sound,

you come
to a place
whose only task

is to trouble you
with tiny
but frightening requests,

conceived out of nowhere
but in this place
beginning to lead everywhere.

RESOURCES

Chapter 1

Buron, K. *When My Worries Get Too Big! A Relaxation Book for Children Who Live with Anxiety*. Shawnee Mission, KS: Autism Asperger Publishing Company, 2006.

Goleman, D. *Destructive Emotions: A Scientific Dialogue with the Dalai Lama*. New York: Bantam Dell, 2003.

Lerner, H. *The Dance of Anger: A Woman's Guide to Changing the Patterns of Intimate Relationships*. New York: HarperCollins, 2005.

Spadaro, P. *Honor Yourself: The Inner Art of Giving and Receiving*. Bozeman, MT: Three Wings Press, 2009.

Chapter 2

Brennan, B., and J. Smith. *Hands of Light: A Guide to Healing Through the Human Energy Field*. New York: Bantam, 2011. Kindle e-book.

Bruyere, R. *Wheels of Light: Chakras, Auras, and the Healing Energy of the Body*. New York: Fireside, 1994.

Chiasson, A. M. *Energy Healing: The Essentials of Self-care*. Louisville, CO: Sounds True, 2013.

Eden, D., and D. Feinstein. *Energy Medicine: Balancing Your Body's Energies for Optimal Health, Joy, and Vitality*. New York: Tarcher, 2008.

Joy, W. *Healing with Body Energy*. New York: Macmillan Audio, 1987. Audible audio edition, abridged.

Weil, A., and A. M. Chiasson. *Self-healing with Energy Medicine*. Louisville, CO: Sounds True, 2009. Audio CD.

Zighelboim, J. *To Health: The New Humanistic Oncology*. Charleston, SC: Booksurge, 2007.

Chapter 3

Conger, C., and M. Stearns. *Sacred Pool*. Santa Monica, CA: CDBY, 2001. Audio CD.

Conger, C., and M. Stearns. *Vision Quest*. Santa Monica, CA: CDBY, 2001. Audio CD.

Davich, V. *The Best Guide to Meditation*. New York: Renaissance Media, 1998.

Hanh, T. N. *The Long Road Turns to Joy: A Guide to Walking Meditation*. Berkeley, CA: Parallax Press, 1996.

Heart, B., and M. Larkin. *The Wind Is My Mother: The Life and Teachings of a Native American Shaman*. New York: Berkley Publishing, 1998.

Kabat-Zinn, J., and R. Davidson. *The Mind's Own Physician: A Scientific Dialogue with the Dalai Lama on the Healing Power of Meditation*. Oakland, CA: New Harbinger Publications, 2011.

Kaplan, A. *Jewish Meditation: A Practical Guide*. New York: Pantheon Books, 1985.

Klipper, M., and H. Benson. *The Relaxation Response*. New York: HarperCollins, 2000.

Kornfield, J. *Guided Meditations for Self-healing*. Louisville, CO: Sounds True, 2011. Audio CD.

Koyiyumptewa, S., C. Davis, and the Hopi Cultural Preservation Office. *The Hopi People (Images of America)*. Charleston, SC: Arcadia Publishing, 2009.

Neihardt, J. *Black Elk Speaks: Being the Life Story of a Holy Man of the Oglala Sioux, the Premier Edition*. New York: State University of New York Press, 2008.

Salzberg, S. *Real Happiness: The Power of Meditation*. New York: Workman Publishing Company, 2011.

Stern, A. *Everything Starts from Prayer: Mother Teresa's Meditations on Spiritual Life for People of All Faiths*. Ashland, OR: White Cloud Press, 2000.

Suzuki, S., and D. Chadwick. *Zen Mind, Beginner's Mind*. Boston: Shambhala Publications, 2011.

Chapter 4

Stone, H., and S. Stone. *Embracing Ourselves: The Voice Dialogue Manual*. Novato, CA: Nataraj Publishing, 1998.

Stone, H., and S. Stone. *Embracing Your Inner Critic: Turning Self-criticism into a Creative Asset*. New York: HarperCollins, 1993.

Stone, H., and S. Stone. *Partnering: A New Kind of Relationship*. Novato, CA: Nataraj Publishing, 2000.

Stone, S. *The Shadow King: The Invisible Force That Holds Women Back*. Lincoln, NE: iUniverse, 2000.

Voice Dialogue International: http://delos-inc.com/

Chapter 5

Dalai Lama, H. H., and V. Chan. *The Wisdom of Compassion: Stories of Remarkable Encounters and Timeless Insights*. New York: Riverhead Books, 2012.

Dass, R. *Be Love Now: The Path of the Heart*. New York: HarperOne, 2011.

Joy, W. *Joy's Way: A Map for the Transformational Journey*. Los Angeles: J. P. Tarcher, 1979.

Shimoff, M., M. Williamson, and C. Kline. *Love for No Reason: 7 Steps to Creating a Life of Unconditional Love*. New York: Free Press, 2010.

Chapter 6

Dass, R. *Remember: Be Here Now*. San Cristobal, NM: Hanuman Foundation, 1971.

Tolle, E. *The Power of Now: A Guide to Spiritual Enlightenment*. Novato, CA: New World Library, 2004.

Chapter 7

The Upaya Institute and Zen Center, in Santa Fe, N.M., founded by Joan Halifax, offers end-of-life care training for professionals, as well as programs for people who are dying or living with a life-changing illness.

Another organization based on the Buddhist tradition of compassion is the Metta Institute, in San Francisco, founded by Frank Osta-seski. It provides educational and professional training for end-of-life care. They too focus on the integration of the spiritual dimensions of living, dying, and transformation. Volunteers run their affiliated Zen Hospice, a center where people reside to receive palliative care and emotional and spiritual support in their final months.

One of the first organizations dedicated to the needs of the dying is the Shanti Project, founded by Charles Garfield. It's a nonprofit human services agency with offices in San Francisco and Los Angeles, providing peer support and guidance to people affected by HIV/AIDS, cancer, and other life-threatening illnesses.

Other compassionate projects that address the needs of the dying are:
An excellent online course: http://www.dyingintolove.com

Education and practical help for the dying: http://www.doorwayin tolight.org

Conscious living, conscious dying: http://livingdying.org

National Hospice and Palliative Care Organization: http://www .nhpco.org/

Alman, B., and P. Lambrou. *Self-Hypnosis: The Complete Manual for Health and Self-Change*. Philadelphia: Brunner/Mazel, 1992.

Callanan, M. *Final Gifts: Understanding the Special Awareness, Needs, and Communications of the Dying*. New York: Bantam, 1992.

Halifax, J., and I. Bycock. *Being with Dying: Cultivating Compassion and Fearlessness in the Presence of Death*. Boston: Shambhala Publications, 2008.

Kabat-Zinn, J. *Mindfulness Meditation for Pain Relief: Guided Practices for Reclaiming Your Body and Your Life*. Louisville, CO: Sounds True, 2009. Audio CD.

Kessler, D. *The Needs of the Dying: A Guide for Bringing Hope, Comfort, and Love to Life's Final Chapter*. New York: Quill, 2000.

Chapter 8

Enright, R. *Forgiveness Is a Choice: A Step-by-Step Process for Resolving Anger and Restoring Hope*. Washington, DC: APA Life Tools, 2001.

Jampolsky, G., and D. Walsch. *Forgiveness, the Greatest Healer of All*. Hillsboro, OR: Beyond Words Publishing, 1999.

Kornfield, J. *The Art of Forgiveness, Lovingkindness, and Peace*. New York: Bantam Dell, 2008.

www.forgiving.org/

www.geraldjampolsky.com

www.jackkornfield.com

Chapter 9

Bosnak, R. *Embodiment: Creative Imagination in Medicine, Art, and Travel*. New York: Routledge, 2007.

Chodron, P. *When Things Fall Apart: Heart Advice for Difficult Times*. Boston: Shambhala Publications, 2002.

Gawain, S. *Creative Visualization: Use the Power of Your Imagination to Create What You Want in Your Life*. Novato, CA: New World Library, 2002.

Johnson, R. *Inner Work: Using Dreams and Active Imagination for Personal Growth*. New York: HarperCollins, 1989.

Jung, C. G.. *Jung on Active Imagination*. Edited by J. Chodorow. Princeton, NJ: Princeton University Press, 1997.

Liu, E., S. Noppe-Brandon, and Lincoln Center Institute. *Imagination First: Unlocking the Power of Possibility*. San Francisco: Jossey-Bass, 2009.

Rinpoche, S., P. Gaffney, and A. Harvey. *The Tibetan Book of Living and Dying*. San Francisco: HarperCollins, 1992.

Suzuki, D. T., and C. Jung. *An Introduction to Zen Buddhism*. New York: Grove Press, 1994.

Von Franz, M. *Alchemical Active Imagination: Revised Edition*. Boston: Shambhala Publications, 1979.

Chapter 10

Aizenstat, S. *Dream Tending: Awakening to the Healing Power of Dreams*. New Orleans: Spring Journal, 2011.

Bosnak, R. *A Little Course in Dreams*. Boston: Shambhala Publications, 1986.

Garfield, P. *Creative Dreaming: Plan and Control Your Dreams to Develop Creativity, Overcome Fears, Solve Problems, and Create a Better Self*. New York: Fireside, 1995.

Garfield, P. *Your Child's Dreams*. New York: Ballantine, 1984.

Mindell, A., and A. Mindell. *Coma: The Dreambody Near Death*. Portland, OR: Lao Tse Press, 2009.

Taylor, J. *Dream Work: Techniques for Discovering the Creative Power in Dreams*. Mahwah, NJ: Paulist Press, 1983.

Von Franz, M. *On Dreams and Death*. Boston: Shambhala Publications, 1986.

An integrative health retreat focused on the healing potential of dreaming: http://www.santabarbarahealingsanctuary.com

Online dream sharing: http://www.cyberdreamwork.com and http://www.dreamgate.com

International Association for the Study of Dreams: http://www.asdreams.org

Chapter 11

Daniel, L. *How to Write Your Own Life Story: The Classic Guide for the Nonprofessional Writer*. Chicago: Chicago Review Press, 1997.

Spence, L. *Legacy: A Step-by-Step Guide to Writing Personal History*. Athens, OH: Swallow Press/Ohio University Press, 1997.

A private, personalized site for you to keep family and friends up-to-date during a health event: http://www.caringbridge.org

Afterword

Bennet, S. *Wisdom Walk: Nine Practices for Creating Peace and Balance from the World's Spiritual Traditions*. Novato, CA: New World Library, 2007.

Byock, I. *The Best Care Possible: A Physician's Quest to Transform Care Through the End of Life*. New York: Penguin, 2012.

Levine, S., and O. Levine. *Who Dies? An Investigation of Conscious Living and Conscious Dying*. New York: Anchor Books, 1989.

Wilber, K. *Grace and Grit: Spirituality and Healing in the Life of Treya Killam Wilber*. Boston: Shambhala Publications, 1991.

Ancient wisdom ceremonial council site: http://rootsandwingsfoundation.org

Music for Healing and Meditation

Adams, P. *Flute Meditations for Dreaming Clouds*. Peoria, IL: Lakefront, 2007. Audio CD.

Amaravati. *Mesa*. Hemel Hempstead, UK: Amaravati, 2009. Audio CD.

Anugama. *Healing*. Kihei, HI: Open Sky Music, 2002. Audio CD.

Anugama. *Shamanic Dream*. Kihei, HI: Open Sky Music, 2002. Audio CD.

Demby, C. *Sacred Space Music*. San Francisco: Hearts of Space Records, 1991. Audio CD.

Deuter. *Spiritual Healing*. Santa Fe, NM: New Earth Records, 2008. Audio CD.

Evenson, D., and Soundings Ensemble. *Eagle River*. Bellingham, WA: Soundings of the Planet, 2005. Audio CD.

Halpern, S. *Deep Alpha: Brainwave Synchronization for Meditation and Healing*. San Anselmo, CA: Inner Peace Music, 2012. Audio CD.

Hovhaness, A. *Celestial Gate*. Orchestra of Flanders. Rudolf Werthen. Cleveland: Telarc, 1995. Audio CD.

Kobialka, D. *Timeless Motion*. San Antonio: Lisem Records, 1998. Audio CD.

Rieger, B. *A Celebration of Life and Love*. Fort Wayne, IN: Mayan Dream Productions International, 2012. Audio CD.

Roach, S. *Quiet Music: The Original 3-Hour Collection*. Brooklyn, NY: Projekt Records, 2011. Audio CD.

Rohani, S. *Beauty of Love*. Pooler, GA: Serenity Records, 2010. Audio CD.

Stearns, M. *Encounter: A Journey in the Key of Space*. San Francisco: Hearts of Space Records, 1991. Audio CD.

Wild, C., and Liquid Mind. *Relax: A Liquid Mind Experience*. Sausalito, CA: Real Music, 2007. Audio CD.

INDEX